DOS CAMINOS
MEXICAN STREET FOOD

DOS CAMINOS
MEXICAN STREET FOOD

120 AUTHENTIC RECIPES TO MAKE AT HOME

SKYHORSE PUBLISHING

IVY STARK with Joanna Pruess

Photography by Battman Studios

Skyhorse Publishing books may be purchased in bulk at special discounts for sales promotion, corporate gifts, fund-raising, or educational purposes. Special editions can also be created to specifications. For details, contact the Special Sales Department, Skyhorse Publishing, 307 West 36th Street, 11th Floor, New York, NY 10018 or info@skyhorsepublishing.com.

Skyhorse® and Skyhorse Publishing® are registered trademarks of Skyhorse Publishing, Inc.®, a Delaware corporation.

Visit our website at www.skyhorsepublishing.com.

10 9 8 7 6 5 4 3 2 1

Library of Congress Cataloging-in-Publication Data
Stark, Ivy.
    Dos Caminos' Mexican street food / Ivy Stark and Joanna Pruess.
        p. cm.
    Includes index.
    ISBN 978-1-61608-279-6 (hardcover : alk. paper)
    ISBN 978-1-62636-124-9 (paperback : alk. paper)
    1. Cookbooks.   2. Cooking, Mexican.   I. Title.
    TX716.M4 S685 2011
    641.5972
                    2011026002

Printed in China

To all of the wonderful Mexican cooks and chefs,
from street stalls to chic restaurants, who have
shared with me their passion and knowledge
of the most intriguing cuisine on earth.

CONTENTS

INTRODUCTION

My Road to Dos Caminos:
A Journey of Two Paths

Most kids dream of adventures, but I was quite lucky: My family took some pretty offbeat vacations to places like Puerta Vallarta and Oaxaca, Mexico, before they became popular tourist destinations. We lived our exciting activities, and meals were amusing or enlightening escapades as well. Many of these experiences colored my approach to eating and cooking in general, and ultimately they led me to Dos Caminos.

For example, I ate my first jalapeño on a Mexicana Airlines flight when I was about five. At seven, my parents ordered frogs' legs for my sister and me. We weren't happy about it, but there was no choice: They really encouraged us to try new things, and this has become a lifelong pursuit. (I actually thought they tasted good, but nonetheless I was grossed out.)

There was an insane Mexican-themed restaurant called Casa Bonita, in Lakewood, Colorado, thirty minutes from where we lived in Boulder, that had a giant waterfall with cliff divers, strolling mariachi groups, a pirate cave, and lots of other wacky elements. Even if the food was marginal, the entertainment value was great and we insisted on going there for all birthdays. As we explored and ate unfamiliar dishes, my curiosity about food and culture grew.

Later adventures often took me back to Mexico, especially the backstreets and little alleyways of places like Puebla, an important culinary center, and more out-of-the-way places, like Teotítlan.

After graduating from college, I attended the Institute of Culinary Education, in New York, and was fortunate to find a career I adore. Combining my classic culinary training and European-style restaurant expe-

riences with my Mexican adventures, I have followed two paths in my career. So, perhaps Dos Caminos—a name that means "two roads"—was my destiny.

As the executive chef of a group of restaurants called Dos Caminos, I speak directly with our guests through my food. But I also convey my (and the restaurants') passion on television and in appearances at charity events. In one way or another, each allows me to show that the Mexican street food at Dos Caminos reflects how we want to eat today: food that is tasty, unpretentious, and meant for sharing.

That said, I think it's important to distinguish between street food and fast food. While shortcuts can be taken in Mexican cooking, there is great pride and history in the foods found on the street. A lot of these dishes in fact are really "slow foods" that are braised and stewed over time to allow their complex flavors to develop. They have been celebrated for centuries. If I have modified some of them for today's dining style, they remain true to the spirit of the vibrant, colorful cuisine of Mexican streets that so many Dos Caminos customers love.

So how did I get here?

If it was my mom who showed me how cooking could magically transform ordinary ingredients into special foods, it was my dad's work in hotels—including going to restaurant shows with their spectacular ice carvings and elaborate displays—that first tempted me to look in the back of the house to see how it all worked.

Mom designed kitchens professionally, but it seemed to me that she didn't particularly enjoy cooking. At home, my family ate dishes like spaghetti and meatballs or steak and potatoes. I love them, but they are not what you'd call exotic.

Still, I clearly remember one Saturday afternoon when I was about five: we were in our big, old-fashioned kitchen mixing warm potatoes with homemade mayonnaise and then tasting the results. It was one of those lightbulb moments that remain as clear as if it were yesterday. Even today I get a shiver of excitement when I recall that potato salad. It's the same feeling I have now when I see perfect asparagus in the market or a new dish that I am particularly proud of as it goes out of the kitchen for the first time.

Many subsequent Saturday afternoons were spent destroying our kitchen with my first and still-beloved *Pooh Cookbook*. My favorite recipe was Popovers for Piglet. Somehow, I was always amazed when the egg batter became an airy, hollow roll that unfailingly "popped" out of the muffin tin.

By eight, cooking had captured my interests and taste buds.

I even made my mother fib about my age to get me into a cooking class for nine-year-olds at the YMCA. (I was months shy of that age.) From *Pooh* I graduated to *The Betty Crocker Cookbook* and its amazing cake recipes. I'm still a big fan of baking cakes and often do it to relax on the weekend.

The Joy of Cooking and *Mastering the Art of French Cooking* came next. My high school friends were my test subjects, and I owe them a debt of gratitude for their willingness to try things like *escargots* and *îles flottantes* (floating islands) to perfect my techniques.

Why Mexican cooking?

That's probably the question I'm most often asked, usually phrased as something like, "What's a blonde American girl doing cooking Mexican food?" The answer is simple: I fell in love.

After high school in Boulder, I moved to Los Angeles to attend UCLA. There I met Jorge. Because Mexicans are all about their families, not long after Jorge came into my life, I was introduced to his charming *mamacita*, Alegría, and her cooking.

I certainly wasn't a stranger to Mexican food, having grown up in Colorado with its large Mexican American population and proximity to Mexico, and with parents who were fearless eaters and travelers.

But her food was nothing like what I'd tasted at Casa Bonita, in Denver, and I knew I had to learn it! Strangely, that notion had never occurred to me before.

I planted myself at Alegría's side every single free moment I had, and she generously shared all of her wonderful recipes with me. How fortunate I was since many cooks are very protective of their recipes and culinary secrets.

Soon I began spending more time with Alegría than I did with Jorge!

My passion becomes a profession.

Once I graduated from UCLA with my history degree in hand, my sister Holly and I booked a lightning tour of Europe on a Eurail Pass. We ate very well indeed. Our inaugural pizza in Rome had me smitten with the gorgonzola and it sealed my future career. It still has its way with me decades later in my dreams of Italy.

When I returned, I headed to New York City to study classic French cuisine at Peter Kump's Cooking School (now the Institute for Culinary Education). After graduation came the required externship. While the idea of working in some of the greatest kitchens in the world was tempting, I was drawn back to Los Angeles by the Mexican foods I'd come to love. At that time, they simply didn't exist in New York.

At the Border Grill in Santa Monica, chefs and co-owners Mary Sue Milliken and Susan Feniger introduced me to their contemporary approach to preparing Mexican food with fresh farmers' market vegetables, day boat–caught fish, and creative flair. Mary Sue and Susan are also great lovers of street food, and many of their inspirations come from streets around the world. Soon, I was enamored of street food as well. Finally, it was at the Border Grill where I met Scott Linquist, my best friend, colleague, and indispensable collaborator.

Eventually I returned to New York and spent many years refining my skills at some of the best restaurants in the city, including the Sign of the Dove and Cena. But Mexican cooking seemed like my destiny. I wanted to give the cuisine the respect I thought it deserved, so it became the focus of my career. Although I've taken some interesting detours (Mediterranean food at Amalia and Japanese food in Beijing, China), the food and culture of Mexico remain my true love.

A Mexican street food cookbook.

While there are plenty of Mexican cookbooks, one subject that has been overlooked is the street food of Mexico that is such a vibrant, flavorful, and significant part of the cuisine. I've been snacking from the carts in Mexico practically all of my life and have long wanted to share my passion for these delicious and often surprisingly complex foods at Dos Caminos and now with a broader audience through this book. Every cart or market stall is a new adventure; I'm constantly amazed at the variety and ingenuity of the cooks who are intensely proud of what they do and light up at the declaration, ¡*Que rica*!

In this book you'll find recipes straight from the street and others adapted to the table. They are simple, they are colorful, and—hopefully—they will encourage you to explore and experiment with the remarkable ingredients of Mexico in your kitchen. Many—like dried and canned chiles, prepared *masa*, and Mexican chocolate—can be stored for weeks at a time in your pantry and brought out to use with fresh meat, seafood, and vegetables to prepare an exciting Mexican dinner at any time.

Cooking Mexican food can be simple enough for a family dinner or a fun evening with friends. Much of the work for enticing appetizers, salsas, side dishes, and even complicated mole sauces can be done ahead of time. To make things easier, you'll find step-by-step photos of unfamiliar techniques, a glossary of terms, and a discussion of the special equipment that is sometimes used. At the end of this book is a list of resources for purchasing the ingredients in the book, as well as suggested substitutions that you can use to simplify or create a variation on the recipes.

In my travels, I also took pictures and collected recipes and all manner of memorabilia. In sharing these little mementos with you, my wish is that they will transport you to the streets in the towns both small and large of Mexico and provide you with a feeling of having been there with me as I devoured everything with my eyes, nose, and palate.

I hope that this book brings you closer to the beloved street food of Mexico, whether you are new to Mexican cuisine or looking to expand your knowledge. And that like me, you will share these recipes with your family and friends to bring an exciting, zesty cuisine to life for them.

—**Ivy Stark**

Thinking beyond this book . . .

Like all recipes and techniques, those in this book are meant as a guideline to help you start your exploration of Mexican street food. Once you have prepared and savored some of these dishes, I hope you will borrow or adapt some of those ideas to your own cooking.

For example, many of the fresh and cooked salsas in the *"Salsas y Condimentos"* chapter and throughout the book can be used with everyday dishes. Their bold, complex flavors add a lot of style to grilled fish, roast chicken, pasta, or a plain baked potato. Once you try freshly made salsas, you will appreciate how much better they are than most purchased products. While the list of ingredients may look long at first, I think you will quickly get used to soaking dried chiles and reaching for your electric blender, and making them will become almost second nature.

The beloved *mole* sauces (page 29) at the heart of many Mexican foods are made with lots of ingredients and take time to prepare. Even in Mexico they are most often made for celebrations and holidays. Because it's a time-consuming job, I suggest you make the full recipe. Then, once all the toasting and grinding has taken place, and before you add any stock, you have a thick paste that you can scrape into a tightly sealed container and freeze for months. I suggest using small boxes or jars so you defrost only as much as you need for each dish.

Once made, you will be amazed at how many ways you can use *mole*. Not only is a tablespoon of *Mole Negro* used on top of *Sincronizadas* (page 58), but one of my favorite quick snacks is a grilled open-face cheese sandwich on a flour tortilla with a dollop of *Mole Poblano* in the center.

If you have leftover braised or stewed meats, add them to casseroles, layer them in lasagna, or wrapped them in enchiladas. Or combine chopped leftover chicken or meats with a simple sauce to make a tempting hash. There are many possibilities.

EQUIPMENT AND TECHNIQUES
EQUIPO Y TÉCNICAS

Equipment/Equipo

Cazuelas are large, often colorfully painted pots made of pottery or cast iron; typically they are about 6 inches deep with glazed interiors and two handles used for slowly simmering *moles* and other stews.

A **comal** is a large round griddle generally made of aluminum, cast iron, or sometimes clay. It is used to heat tortillas and roast vegetables or chiles. There are newer versions that have a nonstick finish.

An **electric blender**, while not Mexican in origin, is indispensable for grinding ingredients like chiles and herbs for salsas.

Molcajetes are lava-stone mortars that typically stand on three legs. They are used with a *tejolote*, or pestle, to grind spices and to pound avocados into chunky-smooth guacamole.

A **molinillo de madera** is the essential wooden tool that Mexicans use like a whisk to foam milk for hot chocolate and other beverages. It is rotated between two hands, palms together, to make the liquid foamy.

A **plancha** is a flat metal griddle or plate used for grilling food. A large skillet may be used in its place.

A **prensa de tortilla**, or tortilla press, is invaluable in Mexico cuisine. It is usually made of cast iron, wood, or aluminum with a base, top, and handle. To make tortillas, place a small ball of *masa* (cornmeal dough) between the two large round plates or blocks of wood and press them together to flatten it into a disk. To prevent the *masa* from sticking, line both sides with plastic wrap. In Mexico, you also see women using their hands to pat dough into tortillas.

Techniques/Técnicas

Preparing Fresh and Dried Chiles
FRESH CHILES

To Roast Fresh Chiles

- Chiles are roasted in order to remove the thin skin that covers them, as well as to give them a unique, rich flavor. There are several methods, but the most commonly used technique is roasting over direct heat.
- Place the chiles directly over a medium flame on a gas stove. Turn the chiles with tongs until their entire skins are charred, approximately 5 to 10 minutes, depending on the heat of the flame and the size of the chiles. Do not char the chiles too much or the flesh will burn and taste bitter.
- Immediately place the chiles in a plastic bag and close the bag or cover the chiles with a damp cloth and leave for 10 to 15 minutes. This procedure is called "letting the chiles sweat," and it serves two functions: to make the thin skin easier to remove and to let the chiles cook slightly in their own steam.

To Peel Chiles

- Turn on the cold water tap so that a thin stream of water is running out. Hold each roasted chile under the running water and use your fingers to remove the charred skins. If parts of the chiles' skin stick to the chile, use a paring knife to remove them.
- Or you can dip the chiles in a medium-size bowl of water as needed to peel each chile. Do not let them soak or they will lose flavor.

To Remove Membranes and Seeds

- Some sauces and other dishes use chiles with their seeds and membranes intact, but more often, the seeds and membranes are removed, because that's where the heat is concentrated. If the chile is to be used whole and stuffed, do not remove the stem and be careful not to break the skin while cleaning.
- Use a small knife and carefully make a lateral incision in the chile; remove the placenta, which is the small cluster of seeds attached to the base of the stem; also carefully remove the membranes that run the length of the chile.
- Gently rinse the chile and remove any seeds that are still adhering to it.
- If the chile is to be cut into strips, cut a "lid" in the top part of the chile around the stem, and remove. Make a lateral incision, pull open, and remove the seeds and membranes. Rinse.

To Soak Fresh Chiles

- If you find that the chiles are too fiery, you can soak them to remove excess piquancy. Soak the chiles in a mixture of 1 cup water, 1 tablespoon white vinegar, and 2 teaspoons salt (double or triple the amounts depending on the number of chiles). Soak for about 40 minutes.

DRIED CHILES

To Clean Dried Chiles

- Wipe the skin of the chile with a damp cloth to remove impurities. If the chile is going to be used whole and stuffed with a filling, leave the stem on.
- Make a small lateral cut and remove the seeds and membranes. If you are not going to be using the chiles whole, remove the stem and remove seeds. Sometimes chiles are too dry, and when you try to remove the seeds and membranes, they break into small pieces. If that happens, toast and soak the chiles before cleaning them.

To Roast or Toast Dried Chiles

- Chiles are roasted or toasted so that they release their aroma and are easier to grind or purée.
- Heat an iron skillet over medium heat.
- Place the chiles in the hot skillet, using a spatula to press them against it slightly.
- Turn them so that both sides begin to change color. This will take 1 to 2 minutes. Be careful not to burn them.

To Soak Dried Chiles

- Place the chiles in just enough lukewarm water to cover them for 5 to 10 minutes; this softens them and makes them regain body.

To Fry Dried Chiles

- Heat a scant tablespoon of oil in a small skillet.
- Add the chile and fry lightly for a minute, turning to cook both sides.

BASIC TORTILLA MASA

Yield: 1 pound

 Corn tortillas are at the foundation of Mexican cuisine and the center of most Mexican meals. Mexicans love to turn anything on the table into a taco. After some practice, most cooks can do more than one tortilla at a time.

1 ¾ cups *masa harina*
1 ⅛ cups water

 THE FOUNDATION

THE DOUGH FOR TORTILLAS IS
CALLED MASA. THIS REFERS
TO ALL DOUGHS.

1. In a medium bowl, mix together the *masa harina* and hot water until thoroughly combined. Turn the dough onto a clean surface and knead until smooth. If the dough is too sticky, add more *masa harina*; if it is too dry, sprinkle with water. Cover dough tightly with plastic wrap and let it stand for 30 minutes.

2. Preheat a cast-iron skillet or griddle to medium heat.

3. Divide the dough into walnut-sized balls. Using a tortilla press, a rolling pin, two heavy books, or your hands, press each ball of dough flat between two sheets of plastic wrap.

4. Place a tortilla in the preheated pan and cook for approximately 30 seconds, or until slightly browned. Turn the tortilla; cook the second side for about 30 seconds and then transfer to a plate. Repeat the process with each ball of dough.

Keep tortillas covered with a towel to stay warm and moist until ready to serve.

TORTILLAS (STEP BY STEP)

CHAPTER TWO

PICO DE GALLO

Yield: about 1 quart

5 plum tomatoes, finely diced
1 white onion, finely diced
1 bunch cilantro, chopped
3 ounces chile peppers, half *jalapeños*, half *serranos*, minced
Juice of 1 lime
Kosher or fine salt and freshly ground black pepper

1. Combine the tomatoes, onions, cilantro, peppers, and lime juice in a nonreactive bowl; season to taste with salt and pepper. Refrigerate for at least 1 hour before serving to blend the flavors. Can be refrigerated for up to 2 days.

ABOUT SALSA

ALL OF THESE SALSA RECIPES CAN BE DI-
VIDED (OR MULTIPLIED). MEXICANS EAT
SALSA WITH ABANDON, SO WHY NOT MAKE
THE FULL AMOUNT AND KEEP THEM IN YOUR
REFRIGERATOR TO SPICE UP ALL KINDS OF
FOODS? THEY WILL KEEP FOR AT LEAST A
WEEK. ADDITIONAL SALSA AND CONDIMENT
RECIPES APPEAR THROUGHOUT THE BOOK.
AS A GENERAL RULE, FOR A MILDER SALSA,
REMOVE THE SEEDS AND MEMBRANES FROM
CHILES BEFORE USING (AND ALWAYS WEAR
RUBBER GLOVES FOR PROTECTION).

ROASTED TOMATO-CHIPOTLE SALSA

Yield: about 1 quart

10 medium tomatoes
6 cloves garlic
1 medium white onion, sliced
2 to 4 canned *chipotles en adobo*
¼ cup red wine vinegar
Kosher or fine sea salt

1. Preheat the oven to 350°F.

2. On a sheet pan, roast the tomatoes, garlic, and onion until tender and lightly browned, about 15 minutes. Transfer them along with the chiles and vinegar to the jar of an electric blender and purée until smooth.

3. Pour the mixture into a medium-size saucepan and gently simmer for about 20 minutes; season to taste with salt and serve.

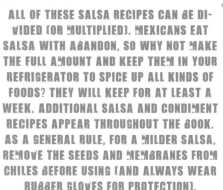 **DOS CAMINOS**
MEXICAN STREET FOOD

ROASTED TOMATO-
SERRANO SALSA

Yield: 1 pint

4 ripe plum tomatoes (about 1 pound)

4 *serrano* chiles

2 medium cloves garlic, unpeeled

1 medium white onion

1 teaspoon freshly squeezed lime juice

1 bunch fresh cilantro, coarse stems removed

Kosher or fine sea salt

1. Preheat the broiler. Position a broiler rack 8 inches from the heat.

2. Broil the tomatoes, chiles, garlic, and onion until blackened all over, turning once.

3. Leave the blackened skin on the vegetables. Transfer all the ingredients to the jar of an electric blender, adding lime juice and cilantro, and pulse until coarsely chopped; season to taste with salt.

SERRANO
SALSA

Yield: 1 quart

1 cup cider vinegar

1 tablespoon sugar

4 whole allspice berries

¼ cup vegetable oil

1 cup minced white onions

16 *serrano* chiles, roasted, peeled, seeded, and diced

1 tablespoon salt

¼ cup freshly squeezed lime juice

1 cup chopped cilantro

1. In small saucepan, combine the vinegar, sugar, and allspice and simmer until the sugar dissolves. Set aside.

2. Heat the oil in a medium-size skillet over medium heat; stir in the onion and cook until translucent, about 4 minutes. Add the serranos, allspice-vinegar syrup, and salt and gently simmer until the mixture binds together, 8 to 10 minutes.

3. Cool, fold in the lime juice and cilantro, scrape into a food processor, and process until blended but still slightly chunky. Taste to adjust the salt, if needed.

DOS CAMINOS
MEXICAN STREET FOOD

HOUSE TOMATILLO SALSA

TOMATILLO DE MESA

Yield: 1 quart

¼ pounds tomatillos, husked, washed, and coarsely chopped

4 cloves garlic

1 *serrano* chile

1 *jalapeño* chile

1 small white onion, coarsely chopped

¼ cup chopped cilantro

Kosher or fine sea salt

In the container of a food processor, combine the tomatillos, garlic, *serrano* and *jalapeño* chiles, onion, and cilantro; pulse until chunky-smooth. Pour the salsa through a fine strainer, straining out most of the excess liquid. Transfer to a container, season to taste with salt, and refrigerate for up to 1 day.

TOMATILLO-PASILLA DE OAXACA SALSA

Yield: 2 quarts

2 ½ pounds tomatillos, husked, rinsed, and quartered

1 tablespoon lard or vegetable oil

10 medium cloves garlic

15 small *pasilla de Oaxaca* chiles, stemmed and seeded

Kosher or fine sea salt

1. In a small saucepan, combine the tomatillos with enough water to come about halfway up the side of the pan, cover, and cook over medium heat until they are soft, about 10 minutes; strain, reserving the liquid.

2. Meanwhile, on a plancha or in a heavy skillet, melt the lard over medium heat. Add the garlic and cook until soft and well charred on all sides, 5 to 10 minutes; transfer to the jar of an electric blender.

3. Add the chiles to plancha and toast for 2 minutes per side. Remove, tear them into pieces, and add them to the blender. Pour in the reserved cooking liquid, add a large pinch of salt, and blend until smooth. Add the tomatillos, blend, and taste to adjust the salt, as necessary.

HABANERO SALSA

Yield: 2 ½ cups

The habanero is the hottest of the hot, but beyond the heat is a distinct fruitiness that adds a wonderful spark to almost anything. Besides serving as a spicy salsa for the Gorditas de Res on page 173, it's excellent as a dip for tortilla chips or even spooned on a simple piece of grilled fish. But it's spicy and not for timid taste buds. Removing the seeds and membranes will tame it a little. It's also a nice sauce to combine with fruits, like mango, orange, or pineapple.

8 plum tomatoes, coarsely chopped

5 *habanero* chiles, seeds and membranes removed, if desired

4 cloves garlic, chopped

1 medium white onion, coarsely chopped

1 teaspoon dried oregano, preferably Mexican

⅓ cup finely chopped cilantro, with thick stems removed

Salt and freshly ground black pepper

In the container of a food processor, combine the tomatoes, chiles, garlic, onion, and oregano; pulse until fairly finely chopped. Add cilantro and pulse to blend; season to taste with salt and pepper. Scrape the salsa into a nonreactive bowl, cover, and refrigerate.

HABANERO SALSA II

Yield: 1 quart

3 cups water

3 cups white vinegar

3 *habanero* chiles, cut in half, seeds and membranes removed

3 bay leaves

2 shallots, cut in half

2 cloves garlic

4 carrots, cut in half

1 yellow bell pepper, cut in half, seeds and membranes removed

1 tomato

Salt

This is one of our table sauces at Dos Caminos. The previous version is a more traditional tomato-based salsa. This one is a lighter, contemporary take that uses carrots to counter the heat of the habanero. The two recipes are quite different, so use the one that appeals to you.

1. In a nonreactive pot, combine the water, vinegar, chiles, bay leaves, shallots, garlic, carrots, bell pepper, and tomato; bring to a boil over medium-high heat and cook until the peppers are tender, about 10 minutes, and strain. Reserve the liquid.

2. Transfer the strained mixture to an electric blender. Start by adding ½ cup of the liquid, adding more as needed to make a smooth sauce, and purée. Stir until blended; strain again and season to taste with salt. Cool and store in the refrigerator until needed.

CHILES
TORREADOS

Yield: 2 ½ cups

This basic condiment is found on tables in almost every casual taquería and eatery in Mexico. It is surprisingly similar to some that might be found on Asian tables.

½ cup olive oil

24 *serrano* chiles

1 red onion, sliced

8 cloves garlic, thinly sliced

¼ cup Maggi sauce (see "Ingredients," page 273)

Juice of 4 limes

Salt

Heat the oil in a large skillet over medium-high heat; add the chiles and sauté until they begin to blister. Add the onion and cook, stirring occasionally, until soft; stir in the garlic and cook until soft and golden. Add the Maggi sauce and lime juice and simmer until the flavors are combined and liquid is slightly reduced; season to taste with salt.

THREE-COLORED PICKLED PEPPERS

RAJAS TRES COLORES

Yield: 1 quart

2 tablespoons olive oil

1 medium red onion, thinly sliced

4 cloves garlic, thinly sliced

2 red bell peppers, roasted, peeled, seeded, and cut into thin strips

2 yellow bell peppers, roasted, peeled, seeded, and cut into thin strips

2 *poblano* chiles, roasted, peeled, seeded, and cut into thin strips

¼ cup sherry vinegar

2 tablespoons freshly squeezed lime juice

1 tablespoon Maggi sauce or Worcestershire sauce

1 teaspoon kosher salt

Heat the oil in a large skillet over medium-high heat; add the onions and sauté until lightly browned, about 5 minutes, then add the garlic and sauté for 1 more minute, stirring frequently. Stir in the pepper and chile strips and mix thoroughly. Pour in the vinegar, lime juice, and Maggi sauce, lower the heat, and simmer for 5 minutes, stirring occasionally; season to taste with salt and refrigerate.

BARBECUE ADOBO

Yield: 1 pint

This would typically be used when pit-roasting a whole animal in Mexico, but at home it can be used as a general meat and poultry marinade.

2 avocado leaves, toasted (page 272)

6 black peppercorns

3 bay leaves

1 clove

1 teaspoon oregano, preferably Mexican

1 teaspoon cumin seeds, toasted

3 *ancho* chiles, stemmed, seeded, and toasted

3 *guajillo* chiles, stemmed, seeded, and toasted

2 tomatillos, roasted

2 tablespoons vegetable oil

6 cloves garlic

1 medium white onion

½ cup cider vinegar

½ cup orange juice

Salt

1. Combine the avocado leaves, peppercorns, bay leaves, clove, oregano, and cumin seeds in a spice grinder or clean coffee mill and grind until fine.

2. In the jar of an electric blender, purée the *ancho* and *guajillo* chiles and the tomatillos until smooth.

3. Heat the oil in a medium-size saucepan over medium heat; add the onion and sweat until soft. Add the chile-tomatillo purée and ground spices and continue to cook for about 5 minutes, stirring constantly. Stir in the vinegar and orange juice and simmer for 20 minutes.

4. Scrape into the blender and purée until smooth; season to taste with salt and cool.

PASTOR MARINADE

Yield: 3 cups

This "shepherd's" marinade is what you'll typically find dripping from the spits of juicy pork roasting in the stalls that surround the zócalo in Puebla. We use this basic marinade with fish, pork, and poultry.

3 *ancho* chiles and 3 *guajillo* chiles (or substitute ½ cup *ancho* chile powder mixed with 2 cups warm water)

4 cloves garlic

1 medium white onion, quartered

4 bay leaves

1 teaspoon chopped fresh thyme leaves

1 teaspoon ground cumin

1 teaspoon dried oregano, preferably Mexican

1 teaspoon freshly ground black pepper

½ teaspoon ground clove

½ teaspoon ground allspice

½ teaspoon ground cinnamon

2 cups water

½ cup cider vinegar, red wine vinegar, or white wine vinegar

1. Remove the stems and seeds from the chiles. Put them in a small saucepan with enough water to cover, bring to a simmer, and let them cool in the liquid.

2. Drain the chiles; transfer them with all of the other ingredients to the jar of an electric blender and purée until smooth. Scrape into a covered container and refrigerate for up to 2 weeks or freeze.

MOLE/MOLE

There are other mole sauces throughout this book.

Mole is the generic name for several sauces used in Mexican cuisine, as well as dishes based on these sauces. In Mexican Spanish, the term, derived from Nahuatl *mulli* or *molli*, means "sauce" or "mixture." It is more general than most people, including culinary experts outside of Mexico, believe, and the ingredients used in making *moles* can be quite dissimilar to each other.

The most well-known versions are from the states of Puebla and Oaxaca. Not only is Puebla's *mole poblano* popular throughout the country, it is the *mole* most people in the United States think of when asked about it. Oaxaca's seven famous *moles* include *Mole Negro, Mole Coloradito*, and *mole chichilo*, known as the legendary seventh *mole* (*see "Chichilo Oaxaqueño" on page 180*). The recipe for *Mole de Xico* from Veracruz, another regional *mole*, is offered on page 41. *Guacamole*, a combined form of the words meaning "avocado mixture/sauce," is found in chapter 5.

All *moles* use numerous ingredients, some more than thirty, and require time to prepare, including roasting chiles, grinding nuts, and long, slow cooking to allow the complex flavors to develop. Because of this, *moles* are generally prepared for celebrations such as weddings and holidays. In *mole poblano*, the dried chiles are commonly *ancho*, *pasilla*, *mulato*, and *chipotle*; the ground nuts and seeds typically include almonds, indigenous peanuts, and sesame seeds along with spices and dried fruits, a small amount of Mexican chocolate, salt, and a variety of other ingredients including charred avocado leaves.

Various stories exist about the invention of *mole*, but none of them are generally accepted, as no good evidence exists to verify them. The most popular has Sor (Sister) Andrea de la Asunción, the cook of the Convent of Santa Rosa, in Puebla de Los Angeles, creating *mole* for the visit of an important archbishop or politician during the 1680s. Another involves Fray (Brother) Pascual who, while similarly preparing a grand dinner for the archbishop, supposedly knocked a tray of spices into the *cazuela* in which a turkey was cooking, accidentally creating *mole poblano de guajalote*, the mouthwatering dish that is considered Mexico's national dish.

The true story of mole will probably never be known since the first published *mole* recipes did not appear until more than one hundred years after these events took place, and after the War of Independence from Spain.

Culinary anthropologists point to *mole* as a symbol of *mestizaje*, the racial mixing of indigenous Mexican people with the Europeans. When Columbus returned to Spain with indigenous foods like corn, tomatoes, squash, chile peppers, and chocolate, it changed Old World cuisines forever; in the same way, Europeans introduced numerous spices to Mexico that, in the case of *mole poblano*, were combined with American turkeys, chiles, and chocolate.

Dark, thick *mole poblano* is the most recognized form of the sauce, and it is the version we serve at Dos Caminos with our Dos Enchiladas. But it is certainly not the only one. *Moles* can range from dark and thick to soup-like and bright green, with red, yellow, and black *moles* each claiming aficionados in different regions.

Mexico's ethnic groups, each its unique culinary tradition, don't necessarily conform to political boundaries and many different *moles* may appear in the same state. In small towns and villages, there are also unique variations. For example, in Teotilán, Oaxaca, the village *mole*, called *mole de castilla*, is strongly flavored with oregano. Mexican geography, with its long mountain ranges, also plays a part in these variations. Oaxaca, for example, is so broken up by mountains that even within the same state there are several different microclimates and culinary regions.

The southern Mexican chicken and fruit stew *mole manchamanteles* translates as "tablecloth stainer" for its deep ruby color from red chiles. *Oaxaqueños* consider it to be one of the seven moles of Oaxaca, although *poblanos* insist it originated in Puebla. (While both states claim the same dish, it may have originated with the most northern of the *Mixteca* people who inhabit the *mixteca poblana* region in what is now southern Puebla and northern Oaxaca.)

MOLE COLORADITO

Yield: 1 gallon

21 *guajillo* chiles, stemmed and seeded

18 *ancho* chiles, stemmed and seeded

2 black peppercorns

2 whole cloves

1 whole allspice berry

1 (1-inch) piece *canela* (Mexican cinnamon)

1 small white onion, quartered

½ small head garlic, cloves separated

8 cups chicken stock, divided

1 pound ripe tomatoes, quartered

1 sprig marjoram or Mexican oregano, or ½ teaspoon dried oregano

2 tablespoons plus 1 teaspoon vegetable oil, divided

½ ripe plantain, peeled and sliced

½ *bolillo* or French roll, sliced

1 tablespoon raisins

5 whole unpeeled almonds

½ cup sesame seeds

3 tablespoons lard or vegetable oil

2 (3-ounce) tablets Mexican chocolate, broken in pieces, or to taste

Salt

1. In a large saucepan, bring 2 quarts of water to a boil. On a 10-inch dry comal or griddle, or in a cast-iron skillet, toast the chiles on both sides over low heat until their skins start to blister and they give off their aroma, about 10 minutes, toasting the anchos a bit slower and longer because of their thicker skins.

2. Transfer the chiles to a medium bowl, cover with boiling water, and soak for 20 minutes, turning to soften them. Using a slotted spoon, transfer the chiles to the jar of an electric blender and purée, using as little of the chile water as possible, about 1 cup. Pass the purée through a strainer or food mill to remove the skins. Set aside.

3. On the comal, griddle, or skillet, toast the peppercorns, clove, allspice, and cinnamon stick; remove. Quickly grill the onion and garlic, turning them often until they become translucent; cool and then transfer them along with the spices to the jar of an electric blender with ½ cup of the chicken stock and purée. Set aside.

4. In an 8-inch cast-iron skillet over medium heat, cook the tomato pieces and marjoram or oregano without oil until condensed, 10 to 15 minutes. First they will give off their juices and then they will dry out. Purée the tomato mixture in the blender, then pass it through a strainer or food mill.

5. In a medium skillet, heat 2 tablespoons of the oil over medium heat; add the plantain and bread slices and fry until

brown, about 12 minutes, and remove. Add more oil, if needed, and fry the raisins until they are plump, about 3 minutes; remove. Add the almonds and fry until light brown, about 4 minutes. Remove.

6. Combine the plantain, fried bread, raisins, and almonds in the blender with 1 ½ cups of the stock and blend until smooth. Wipe out the skillet and return to low heat. Add 1 teaspoon of oil and the sesame seeds and fry until brown, about 2 minutes, stirring constantly; cool the seeds and grind in a *molcajete* or spice grinder.

7. In a heavy 6-quart stockpot, heat 1 tablespoon of the lard over high heat until smoking. Add the chile purée a little at a time, stirring constantly. It will splatter a bit, but keep stirring. Lower the heat to medium and, after about 20 minutes, or when the chile purée is thick, add the tomato mixture and continue to cook for about 15 minutes, stirring to keep the mole from sticking or burning.

8. Stir in the onion and ground spice mixture; add the puréed plantain mixture and the ground sesame seeds, stirring constantly, about 10 minutes. Add 4 ½ to 5 cups

chicken stock to thin the sauce; add the chocolate, stirring constantly. Once the chocolate dissolves, add the salt and let the mole reduce for 30 minutes, stirring occasionally. The more time it has to cook, the better. The chiles should completely lose their bitterness. If needed, add more stock. The mole should be shiny and just thick enough to coat a spoon, but no more.

 ## TIME SAVING

IN EACH MOLE RECIPE, THERE IS A STEP WHEN YOU GRIND ALL THE INGREDIENTS INTO A PASTE. AT THIS POINT, THE MOLE PASTE CAN BE FROZEN FOR SEVERAL MONTHS IN A WELL-SEALED CONTAINER.

MOLE NEGRO

Yield: 2 quarts

1 pound *ancho* chiles

½ pound *guajillo* chiles

½ pound dried *cascabel* chiles

½ pound *chihuacle negro* chiles

2 pounds tomatoes, chopped

1 pound tomatillos, husked, rinsed, and chopped

Vegetable oil

4 slices white bread, cut into cubes

5 cloves

5 whole peppercorns

1 (4-inch) stick *canela* (Mexican cinnamon)

1 sprig fresh thyme

1 pinch cumin

½ cup sesame seeds

½ cup blanched almonds

½ cup shelled peanuts

½ cup walnuts

½ cup raisins

1 ½ plantains, peeled and chopped

1 small white onion, roasted and chopped

1 small clove garlic, roasted and minced

1 corn tortilla

1 (3-ounce) piece Mexican chocolate

½ cup, plus 2 ½ cups additional chicken stock

3 tablespoons lard or vegetable shortening

Salt

1. In a heavy skillet or on the comal, toast the chiles over low heat on both sides until their skins start to blister and they give off their aroma, about 10 minutes, toasting the anchos a bit slower and longer because of their thicken skins. Remove, stem, seed, and devein; set aside.

2. In a large saucepan, combine the tomatoes and tomatillos with enough water to come halfway up the side of the pan and bring to a boil. Drain; transfer to the jar of an electric blender or food processor and purée until smooth. Set aside.

3. In the same pan, add enough oil to measure ½ inch deep. Heat over low heat, add the bread cubes, and fry until golden brown, turning to cook all sides. Add the cloves, peppercorns, *canela*, thyme, and cumin. Stir in the sesame seeds, almonds, peanuts, walnuts, raisins, and plantains, adding more oil as necessary to lightly coat the ingredients lightly. Add the onion and garlic and continue cooking over low heat for 20 minutes; stir in the tomato-tomatillo mixture, remove from heat, and set aside.

4. Cook the tortilla over a flame until dark brown and crispy. Cut up and set aside.

5. In a medium-size skillet, add enough oil to coat the bottom of the pan and heat over medium-high heat until hot. Add the roasted chiles along with toasted tortilla pieces and cook for a few minutes. Scrape them into the large saucepan along with

the tomato-spice-nut mixture. Add the chocolate and cook over low heat until the chocolate has melted. Stir in about ½ cup of stock.

6. Transfer the mixture to the jar of an electric blender or food processor and purée until well blended, adding more of the remaining 2 ½ cups of stock as needed to smooth out the sauce.

7. In a large, deep pot, heat the lard or shortening over medium-high heat. Stir in the purée, add enough chicken stock to achieve the proper consistency, and simmer over low heat for 30 minutes longer, stirring constantly. Pour through a fine strainer and season to taste with salt.

 ## MORE ABOUT MOLE

AMONG MEXICANS, MOLE IS A SOURCE OF GREAT PRIDE, AND FAMILY RECIPES ARE OFTEN SECRETLY HANDED DOWN FROM GENERATION TO GENERATION. A NATIONAL COMPETITION TAKES PLACE EVERY YEAR IN THE TOWN OF SAN PEDRO ATOCPAN, IN THE MILPA ALTA BOROUGH OF MEXICO'S FEDERAL DISTRICT, ON THE SOUTHERN OUTSKIRTS OF MEXICO CITY.

Abigail Mendoza

Whenever I think about Mexican food, the first person who comes to mind is Abigail Mendoza, the owner of Tlamanalli (a Nahuatl word for "offering"), in the tiny village of Teotítlan, Oaxaca. While many people come here for the traditional weavings and to shop for rugs, I've rarely been happier than when luxuriating over a three-hour lunch at the airy, tiled restaurant that Abigail shares with her sisters.

The three women are traditionally dressed with their thick braids interlaced with colorful ribbons and wrapped around their heads. Abigail is the chef and is well known to foodie insiders for cleverly marrying her family's heritage of Zapotec cooking with

her sisters' weaving virtuosity. She was featured on the cover of the first issue of *Saveur* magazine.

While her sisters quietly tended to their looms and yarn-dying, Abigail revealed her secret to making incomparable *mole negro*. She calls it "controlled burning," or toasting all twenty-eight ingredients for just the right length of time. If even one seed is cooked too fast, the *mole* can be bitter. Sesame seeds, for example, are lightly toasted while dried chiles are toasted until almost black. It was an invaluable learning experience for me.

During the lesson, my attention was drawn to the mournful music of a funeral procession in the street and the somber men with downcast eyes and women carrying calla lilies. Although sad, this traditional display of culture enhanced my visit by reminding me of how ancestors are always honored on el Día de los Muertos or the Day of the Dead, the equivalent to Halloween in this region. In homage to Abigail Mendoza and her spectacular *mole*, I prepare it once a year at Dos Caminos.

Here is her handwritten recipe.

"Mole Negro"
(Porción Para 10 Personas)
De:
Abigail Mendoza. Ruiz

Ingredientes

- 3 chiles Guajillos Medianos (2,3 pasilla.)
- 2 chilhuacle Negro Mediano
- 2 Chileancho Mulato Mediano (recipe)
- 2 cucharasside Uva Pasa Seca sin semilla.
- 2 cucharas Soperas de Alendolí (sesame seeds)
- 3 Piezas de clavos criollos grandes (clares)
- 3 Pimientos Gordas criollos (allspice)
- 4 Piezas de Almendras (almonds)
- 3 Rajas de Canela
- 1/8 parte de Nuez Nuscado (nut meg)
- 1 Pan tostado de Trigo (wheat bread)
- 3 Piezas de 3 Dedos de Hiervas de olor
(thyme)Tomillo y criollo. Secos. y Desmenuzadas.
- 2 Piezas de 3 dedos de oregano criollo Seco
- 1 Pieza de 2 dedos de oregano chino
- 1 pedazo Mediano de Gengibre (ginger)
- 1 hoja Mediana de laurel (bay leaves)
- 1 hoja Grande de Aguacate.(avacado leaf)
- 3 Tomates Rojas regulares. criollas
- 8 Piezas de jitomate de Milpa. ó Tomates Verdes,
- 2 cabezas de Ajo Criollo Mediana. abut 1/2" Size
- 2 Cebollas Medianas con Rabo.
- 3 cucharas Soperas de Azúcar
- 1 Pedazo de chocolate
- 1 cuchara Sopera de Manteca de Cerdo ó
  Grasa de pollo ó Aceite de Maíz.
- 6 Tazas de caldo de Guajolote, Gallina ó Cerdo
- 1 pollo entero criollo
- Sal Al Gusto.

20 de octubre 2004

MOLE POBLANO

Yield: 1 gallon

This robust, nutty, and spicy mole comes from the south central state of Puebla and is the mole we serve at Dos Caminos with our Dos Enchiladas. It is also the ideal sauce for mole poblano de guajalote, the famed roast turkey that is Mexico's national dish. Our version includes ancho, pasilla, and mulato chiles; fruits; nuts; spices such as anise and cinnamon; and a touch of Mexican chocolate (page 274).

1 pound lard, divided

10 *mulato* chiles, stemmed and seeded

5 *pasilla* chiles, stemmed and seeded

5 *ancho* chiles, stemmed and seeded

1 cup slivered almonds

1 cup peanuts

½ cup hulled pumpkin seeds

½ cup sesame seeds, lightly toasted

6 cloves garlic

2 white onions, quartered

3 plum tomatoes

3 tomatillos, husked and rinsed

1 ripe plantain, peeled and cut into 1-inch pieces

1 soft sandwich roll, cut into 1-inch cubes (about 1 ½ cups)

4 (6-inch) corn tortillas, cut into sixths

1 teaspoon ground cumin

1 teaspoon freshly ground pepper

½ teaspoon ground *canela* (Mexican cinnamon)

½ teaspoon dried oregano, preferably Mexican

¼ teaspoon ground allspice

¼ teaspoon ground anise

1 (3-ounce) disk Mexican chocolate, finely ground

½ cup finely chopped *piloncillo* or firmly packed dark brown sugar

½ cup dark raisins

½ cup dried apricots

2 quarts chicken stock

Kosher salt

1. In a very large, heavy-bottomed pot, heat all but 2 tablespoons of the lard over medium heat. Add the chiles in batches and fry, turning once, until the skins are blistered, 15 to 20 seconds per side. Remove with a slotted spoon or tongs to a large bowl and set aside.

2. In the same pot, add the almonds, cook until golden, 4 to 5 minutes, stirring occasionally, and remove with a slotted spoon. Repeat with the peanuts, and pumpkin and sesame seeds, transferring them with a slotted spoon to the bowl with the chiles.

3. Stir the garlic and onions into the lard and fry until the onions are soft and golden, about 5 minutes. Transfer to the bowl with the cooked ingredients. Stir in the tomatoes and tomatillos, and fry until they begin to soften and turn brown, 6 to 8 minutes. Transfer with a slotted spoon to the bowl.

4. Add the plantains and cook until golden, 3 to 5 minutes; remove to the bowl. Add the bread and the tortillas, cook until lightly brown and crisp, and transfer to the bowl.

5. In a dry skillet, heat the cumin, pepper, cinnamon, oregano, allspice, and anise over medium heat, tossing continuously, until they smell toasty, 1 to 2 minutes; scrape into the bowl with the other ingredients.

6. Discard the remaining lard in the pot and wipe it clean. Add the reserved 2 table-spoons of lard and heat over medium-high heat.

7. Meanwhile, combine the chocolate, sugar, raisins, and apricots with the other ingredients in the large bowl and toss to-gether. Bring the chicken stock to a simmer. In the jar of an electric blender, add the in-gredients in batches and purée, adding only as much stock as needed so that the blades of the blender will turn and make a smooth paste. Scrape the mixture into the pot, and repeat with the remaining ingredients. Fry the paste for 20 minutes, stirring continu-ously. Add the remaining stock, bring to a simmer, and gently cook for 40 minutes more; season to taste with salt. This sauce should have a thick, rich consistency.

MOLE POBLANO AND WINE

MOLE POBLANO IS A STUNNING PARTNER TO RED WINES. ALTHOUGH THE SAUCE IS USUALLY SLIGHTLY SWEET WITH A TOUCH OF CHOCOLATE AND DRIED FRUIT, AS OUR RECIPE SHOWS, THIS ELEMENT IS BALANCED BY THE STRONG FLAVORS OF THE OTHER INGREDIENTS THAT ENHANCE RATHER THAN INTERFERE WITH WINE PAIRINGS.

SEVERAL WINES PAIR WELL WITH MOLE POBLANO. I RECOMMEND PINOT NOIR FOR ITS SWEETNESS AND BEETY FLAVORS THAT HIGHLIGHT THE NUTTY FLAVORS IN THE DISH. RIOJA'S SPICINESS FINDS EQUIVALENT FLAVORS IN MOLE. AND BOTH CABERNET SAUVIGNON AND ZINFANDEL'S SWEET AND SPICY ELEMENTS BRING OUT THE HOT AND SPICY FLAVORS OF MOLE. BEST OF ALL, THE CHOCOLATE BRINGS OUT ALL RED WINES' FRUIT FLAVORS.

OUR TALENTED SOMMELIER, MOLLY ROY, HAS CRAFTED A WINE LIST AT DOS CAMINOS THAT INCLUDES WELL-CHOSEN WINES, BEERS, AND SPIRITS THAT COMPLEMENT OUR MOLES AND ALL OTHER DISHES. INTERESTINGLY ENOUGH, MEXICAN WINES ARE JUST NOW COMING INTO THEIR OWN, AND WE HAVE ADDED SOME AWARD-WINNING WINES FROM BAJA.

DOS CAMINOS
MEXICAN STREET FOOD

MOLE DE XICO

Yield: 3 quarts

Along with the jalapeño chiles, this mole is the most famous export from Veracruz.

4 ounces *mulato* chiles, seeds and veins removed

2 ounces *pasilla* chiles, seeds and veins removed

Vegetable oil for frying

4 cloves garlic

1 white onion, coarsely chopped

2 quarts chicken or turkey stock, divided

¼ cup whole unblanched almonds

¼ cup unblanched hazelnuts

2 tablespoons pine nuts

2 tablespoons pecans

1 tablespoon sesame seeds

¼ cup pitted prunes

2 tablespoons raisins

1 plantain, peeled and sliced

1 slice day-old bread or roll

1 day-old corn tortilla

1 plum tomato, broiled until soft

1 (1-inch) piece *canela*, crushed

1 teaspoon peppercorns, toasted and crushed

3 tablespoons grated *piloncillo* or firmly packed light brown sugar

1 (3-ounce) tablet Mexican chocolate

2 tablespoons salt

1. In a saucepan, combine the *mulato* and *pasilla* chiles with just enough water to cover; simmer for 5 minutes, then set aside to soak for 10 minutes. Drain well.

2. Heat 1 teaspoon of the oil in a small skillet over medium heat, stir in the garlic and onion, and fry until translucent; scrape them into the jar of an electric blender along with ½ cup of the broth and blend until smooth. Add another cup of broth and the chiles, a few at a time, and blend until the mixture becomes very smooth. You may need to do this in two batches, using just enough broth to loosen the blender blades. Remove and set aside.

3. Wipe out the skillet and add a little more oil. Separately fry the almonds, hazelnuts, pine nuts, pecans, sesame seeds, prunes, raisins, plantains, bread, and tortilla until lightly colored, adding more oil as needed; use a slotted spoon to remove each ingredient so the excess fat is left in the pan.

4. Roughly crush the fried nuts, bread, and tortilla once in a food processor before adding them to blender to avoid overtaxing your blender. Add 2 cups of the broth to the blender and then the fried ingredients in small batches, adding more broth as necessary to prevent the blender blade from locking. Scrape the blended fried ingredients into the chile purée.

5. Combine the tomato, *canela*, and peppercorns and add them to the mole mixture along with the *piloncillo* and chocolate; continue cooking over low heat for about 10 minutes. Add another quart of the broth and continue cooking, stirring often to prevent the mole from sticking to the bottom of the pan, for about 30 minutes.

6. By now the mole should be thick, well seasoned, and have pools of oil forming on the surface.

7. Either set aside to cool and store or continue with your recipe.

CHAPTER FOUR

DIVORCED EGGS
HUEVOS DIVORCIADOS

Yield: Serves 1

¼ cup *Salsa Verde* (page 135)

¼ cup Roasted Tomato-Chipotle Salsa
(page 18)

1 to 2 tablespoons clarified butter

1 tablespoon diced white onion

1 teaspoon minced *serrano* chile

2 large eggs

¼ cup *queso Chihuahua* (page 274)

Rajas Tres Colores (page 25) or strips of
roasted red pepper, to garnish

Chopped cilantro, to garnish

2 warm tortillas

Breakfast cooked and served in a cast-iron skillet is real comfort food. While the dish's name means "divorced eggs," in fact, you get two tasty versions of sunny-side up eggs that live agreeably together. You'll need a 6-inch cast-iron (or other heavy skillet) to make it. We serve the skillets on a large round plate atop a folded black napkin with warm tortillas on the side.

1. Prepare the *Salsa Tomatillo de Mesa* and Roasted Tomato-Chipotle Salsa. Turn on the broiler.

2. Heat a cast-iron skillet over medium-high heat until hot but not smoking, 3 ½ to 4 minutes. Add the butter, onion, and chiles and sauté until the onion is translucent. Crack the eggs into the skillet and sprinkle with salt and pepper.

3. Ladle the *Salsa Verde* into one half of the skillet and Roasted Tomato-Chipotle Salsa into the other half. Top with *queso Chihuahua* cheese and transfer the skillet to the broiler until the cheese is melted and slightly browned. Top with *Rajas Tres Colores* or pepper strips and cilantro. Serve with warm tortillas on the side.

MEXICAN-STYLE EGGS

HUEVOS A LA MEXICANA

Yield: Serves 3 generously

This easy and tasty dish is one of the healthful breakfasts I like to eat before running. Mexicans love salsa and use it abundantly. You can choose almost any salsa in the Salsas y Condimentos chapter or in other recipes in this book to serve on the side. My dad is our family's master breakfast cook. His secret to fluffy eggs is to beat them with a stick blender and a tablespoon of water.

1 tablespoon unsalted butter

1 tablespoon vegetable oil

½ white onion, finely chopped

2 *serrano* chiles, seeds and membranes removed, if desired, thinly sliced

6 large eggs, lightly beaten with 1 tablespoon water

2 plum tomatoes, diced

1 bunch cilantro, coarse stems removed and chopped

Salt

1 ripe avocado, preferably Hass variety, peeled, seeded, and sliced lengthwise

8 (4-inch) corn tortillas

3 to 4 cups salsa of your choice

In a deep skillet, melt the butter and oil over medium-high heat. Add the onion and chiles and sauté until the onion is translucent. Add the eggs and tomato and cook until the eggs are done to your taste, 3 to 4 minutes, stirring constantly to prevent sticking. Add the cilantro, remove from heat, and season to taste with salt. Serve on warm plates topped with avocado slices, with warm tortillas and salsa on the side.

DOS CAMINOS
MEXICAN STREET FOOD

RANCHER'S EGGS
HUEVOS RANCHEROS

Yield: Serves 8

This colorful, delicious dish is an icon of Mexican breakfasts and brunches. At Dos Caminos, we cook the eggs sunny-side up—which is traditional—but whichever way you prefer them will work. The Ranchero Sauce is the notable feature of this dish, so serve a cup per person.

Ranchero Sauce (recipe follows)

4 cups My Refried Beans (page 86), warmed

Vegetable oil, for frying

8 (6-inch) corn tortillas

16 thin slices ham, preferably Serrano

16 large eggs

2 cups *queso fresco*, crumbled

2 avocados, preferably Hass variety, peeled and diced

1. Prepare the Ranchero Sauce (right) and My Refried Beans (page 86).

2. In a skillet, pour in enough oil to measure about 1 inch deep and heat to 375°F on an instant-read thermometer. Cook the tortillas until crisp and golden, turning once. Spread each tortilla with about ½ cup of refried beans. Place each in the center of a plate and top with 2 slices of ham.

3. Cook 2 eggs per portion and place them on the ham. Ladle ¼ to ½ cup Ranchero Sauce over the top, sprinkle with crumbled *queso fresco*, add a few slices of avocado, and serve. Pass the extra sauce at the table.

RANCHERO SAUCE

Yield: Makes 2 quarts

2 tablespoons vegetable oil

1 medium white onion, diced

6 cloves garlic, chopped

¼ cup tomato paste

6 medium tomatoes, roasted

2 canned *chipotles en adobo*

4 cups chicken broth

1 cup crumbled cooked bacon

2 red bell peppers, roasted, seeds and membranes removed, and diced

2 *poblano* chiles, roasted, seeds and membranes removed, and diced

Salt

1. Heat the oil in a medium-size pan over medium heat. Add the onion and sauté until lightly browned, 5 to 6 minutes; stir in the garlic and continue to cook until soft, 2 to 3 more minutes.

2. Stir in the tomato paste and sauté briefly. Add the roasted tomatoes, *chipotles*, and chicken stock; stir to blend and simmer for 10 to 15 minutes. Transfer to the jar of an electric blender and purée until smooth. Stir the bacon and bell and *poblano* peppers into the finished sauce, season to taste with salt, if needed, and keep warm.

TORTILLA CASSEROLE
CHILAQUILES

Yield: Serves 4

Whether for a weekend breakfast or brunch, this classic casserole is commonly eaten after a long night of partying. It's a great way to use up leftovers like chicken, beef, or grilled vegetables; it's also delicious with bacon or chorizo added.

Tortilla chips (about 2 cups per person)

1 cup *crema* or commercial sour cream

1 pound (about 2 cups) grated Mexican cheese, like *queso Chihuahua* or *queso Oaxaca*, or Monterey Jack or cheddar

8 large eggs

GARNISHES

½ cup diced tomatoes

½ cup diced avocado, preferably Hass variety

¼ cup minced red onion

¼ cup chopped cilantro

¼ cup grated *Cotija* cheese

1. Prepare the Roasted Tomato-Chipotle Salsa (page 18) and keep warm. Preheat the oven to 350°F.

2. In a very large skillet, combine 2 to 3 handfuls of chips and ¾ cup of the salsa and toss gently until the chips are covered. Add ½ cup of sour cream and ½ cup of grated cheese and gently stir again. Transfer the skillet to the oven and bake until the mixture is lightly browned and crispy on the edges and soft in the center, about 20 minutes. Remove the pan from the oven, add more sauce, if necessary, and more cheese on top.

3. Meanwhile, cook the eggs sunny-side up, or as you want.

4. To serve: spoon the chilaquiles onto a plate and top with two eggs; garnish with tomato, avocado, red onions, cilantro, and *Cotija* cheese. Serve hot with extra salsa on the side. Repeat for each batch.

 ## MY FAVORITE CHILAQUILES IN OAXACA

INSIDE OAXACA'S MAIN MARKET ARE SEVERAL FOOD STALLS, INCLUDING ABUELITA'S (GRANDMA'S), TO WHICH LOADS OF FARMERS GRAVITATE IN THE EARLY MORNING AFTER BRINGING IN THEIR GOODS. ABUELITA'S SELLS A SPECTACULAR ARRAY OF *MOLES* AND SALSAS, AND THEIR CHILAQUILES MADE WITH FARM FRESH EGGS ARE SIMPLY AMAZING. MY LESSON: IF YOU FIND FARM EGGS, THIS IS A DISH WITH WHICH TO CELEBRATE THEM.

TEPITA-STYLE MIGAS

MIGAS TEPITANA

Yield: Serves 4

At Dos Caminos, we serve this classic Mexican breakfast like they make them in Mexico City: a bread-egg sopa (or soup), rather than the Tex-Mex version with scrambled eggs and tortillas. This dish is often made as a hangover cure using leftover bread, a reminder of its humble origins. (Migas means "crumbs.") I first tasted migas in Tepito, a blue-collar barrio in the Colonia Morelos section of Mexico City, where there have been open-air markets since pre-Hispanic times. There are lines of stalls selling migas to late-night owls.

FOR THE BROTH:

1 tablespoon vegetable oil

2 cloves garlic, sliced

1 white onion, finely diced

4 cups chicken stock

1 *chipotle meco* chile

1 *habanero* chile

½ bunch *epazote*, chopped

Salt and freshly ground black pepper

FOR THE EGGS:

1 (3-ounce) link Mexican chorizo

2 teaspoons vegetable oil

2 tablespoons diced white onion

1 clove garlic, sliced

1 teaspoon sliced *serrano* chiles

8 large eggs, for poaching, plus 1 hard-cooked egg, chopped, for garnish

6 (2-inch) pieces torn day-old or rustic bread, toasted

1 teaspoon chopped *epazote*

1. Make the broth: In a large saucepan, combine the oil, onion, and garlic and sweat over medium heat until translucent. Add the *chipotle* and *habanero* chiles and sauté for 2 minutes more. Add the chicken stock, bring to a simmer, add the ½ bunch *epazote*, and simmer for 30 minutes; season to taste with salt and pepper; strain and reserve.

2. Make the eggs: Sauté the chorizo in a small skillet over medium-high heat until browned and separated into small pieces. Remove with a slotted spoon and set aside. Add enough vegetable oil to the skillet to make about 2 teaspoons and heat until hot. Stir in the onions and garlic and sauté until soft; add the *serrano* chiles and chorizo.

3. Pour the broth into the saucepan and bring to a simmer; drop in the eggs and poach until just set. Add the bread and 1 teaspoon *epazote* and simmer for 1 minute more.

4. In each of 4 soup bowls, serve 2 eggs along with a large ladle of the broth. Garnish with chopped hard-cooked egg and serve.

SINALOA-STYLE DRIED BEEF AND SCRAMBLED EGG TACOS

MACHACADO TACOS CON HUEVOS

Yield: Serves 4 to 6

This is our version of a classic Norteño dish (the area between Northern Mexico and Texas) that's made with dry, shredded beef scrambled with eggs. We make it into breakfast tacos. It's a big breakfast for hearty appetites.

½ cup *Pico de Gallo* (page 18)

Guacamole, to garnish (page 71)

1 teaspoon vegetable oil

1 pound leftover Chile and Beer Braised Brisket (page 189), shredded as finely as possible, or purchased cooked brisket

½ cup chopped tomato

¼ cup finely chopped white onion

1 ½ tablespoons finely chopped cilantro leaves

2 teaspoon minced *serrano* chile

1 dozen large eggs, beaten

Salt and pepper

12 (6-inch) flour tortillas

12 slices aged cheddar cheese

4 limes, cut into quarters

1. Prepare the *Pico de Gallo* and guacamole.

2. In a very large skillet, heat the oil over medium-high heat; add the brisket and brown well, stirring often. Add the *Pico de Gallo* and cook for 1 minute to reduce the liquid slightly; add the tomato, onion, cilantro, and *serrano* chile and sauté for 1 minute more. Add the eggs, season with salt and pepper, and stir until the eggs are just set.

3. Meanwhile, heat a griddle or large skillet over high heat. Lay the tortillas on the griddle, heat one side, turn, put a slice of cheese on each, and let it melt slightly.

4. Fill the tortillas with brisket mixture and fold in half.

5. To serve, line up three tacos on each plate with lime "book ends" and serve with additional *Pico de Gallo* and guacamole.

CREAMY GRITS
SÉMOLINA CON CREMA

Yield: Serves 4 to 6

Grits aren't especially Mexican, but Mexicans eat anything that is corn-based and I think this version goes really well with eggs and salsa. Since my mother is from the South, I've been eating grits all my life. She really likes these, but she's my mother and likes anything I cook.

1 quart milk

1 ½ teaspoons salt, divided

1 cup stone-ground grits

1 large bay leaf

½ cup crème fraîche, sour cream, or Greek yogurt

In a large pot over high heat, bring the milk to a boil. Add 1 teaspoon salt, and whisk in the grits in a slow, steady stream. Switch to a wooden spoon and stir in another ½ teaspoon of salt and the bay leaf. Reduce the heat and simmer until thick and the grits begin to come together and pull away from the sides of the pan, about 45 minutes. Once the grits are cooked, stir in the crème fraîche and season to taste.

CORNMEAL BISCUITS WITH CHEDDAR AND CHIPOTLE

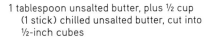

GALLETAS DE QUESO

Makes 12 muffins

These scrumptious, homey biscuits are another influence from my mom. I grew up loving them so I made a Mexican version and serve them with honey butter.

1 tablespoon unsalted butter, plus ½ cup (1 stick) chilled unsalted butter, cut into ½-inch cubes

¾ cup thinly sliced scallions, including most of the green parts

1 ½ cups all-purpose flour

½ cup yellow cornmeal

2 tablespoons sugar

2 ½ teaspoons baking powder

1 teaspoon coarse or kosher salt

½ teaspoon baking soda

1 ½ cups firmly packed, coarsely grated, extra-sharp yellow cheddar cheese

1 large egg, plus 1 egg beaten with 1 table-spoon whipping cream

¾ cup buttermilk

1 tablespoon finely minced canned *chipotle en adobo*

1. Position the rack in center of the oven; preheat to 425°F.

2. Melt the tablespoon of butter in a small nonstick skillet over medium heat. Add the scallions and sauté for 2 minutes to soften slightly; remove from the heat.

3. Combine the flour, cornmeal, sugar, baking powder, salt, and baking soda in the bowl of a food processor. Add the remaining ½ cup butter and pulse until the mixture resembles coarse meal. Add the cheese and pulse just to blend. Scrape into a large bowl.

4. In a glass measuring cup, whisk 1 of the eggs until blended. Add enough buttermilk to measure 1 cup; stir in the scallions and *chipotles*.

5. Make a well in the center of the dry ingredients, pour in the buttermilk mixture, and mix just until evenly moistened. Turn the dough out onto a generously floured surface and knead gently just until the dough holds together, about 10 turns.

6. Pat the dough into a ¾-inch-thick circle and cut out the biscuits using a 2 ½-inch round biscuit cutter. Scrape up leftover dough and re-roll. Transfer the circles to an ungreased baking sheet, spacing them about 1 inch apart. Gather any scraps together and pat again into a disk.

7. Brush the tops of the biscuits with the egg–whipping cream mixture. Bake until golden, a tester inserted into the center comes out clean, and the biscuits feel firm, about 18 minutes. Cool on a rack for 5 minutes and serve warm.

DOS CAMINOS
MEXICAN STREET FOOD

BREAKFAST ROLL
TORTA DESAYUNO

Yield: Serves 1

This breakfast is a favorite of mine. While the recipe is for one, it's easily multiplied to feed a bunch of hungry eaters.

1 whole grain *torta* roll
1 tablespoon unsalted butter, melted
2 slices turkey bacon
Nonstick vegetable spray
2 eggs
1 slice sharp Vermont cheddar cheese
2 slices avocado, preferably Hass variety
3 slices plum tomatoes
Salt and freshly ground black pepper

1. Slice the roll, brush both cut sides with butter, and toast it cut side down in a large skillet until golden; remove. Cook the turkey bacon in the skillet over medium heat until crisp, turning once.

2. Spray a small nonstick skillet with nonstick spray and heat over medium-high heat. Fry the eggs, sunny-side up or whatever you prefer.

3. Put the turkey bacon on the bottom half of the roll. Top with the eggs and then the cheese. Add the avocado and tomato slices and sprinkle with salt and pepper. Put the sandwich together and put it on a griddle or in a pan with a second sprayed pan on top, and cook until the cheese is melted.

HAM AND CHEESE QUESADILLAS

SINCRONIZADAS

Yield: Serves 1

This isn't really a quesadilla—it is cooked flat and then cut into quarters. I like to serve it with Mexican home fries— potatoes sautéed with onions and roasted peppers. Cholula hot sauce is a great addition (page 129). This is the Mexican version of a ham and cheese sandwich, so you can also enjoy it for lunch or as a light supper with a salad, such as the Ensalada de Jicama, Naranja y Manzana on page 74.

1 tablespoon *Mole Negro* (page 34)

Clarified butter, to brush on the griddle or skillet

2 (6-inch) flour tortillas

1 slice Serrano ham

1 ounce grated *queso Chihuahua*

2 large eggs, poached

Guacamole, to garnish

1. Prepare the *Mole Negro*.

2. Brush a griddle or large skillet with butter and heat over high heat; lay a tortilla on the griddle, add the ham and cheese, and top with the other tortilla. Lightly brush the top tortilla with butter. Cook on both sides until brown and crisp and the cheese is melted. Remove, cut in quarters, and serve topped with the poached eggs, *Mole Negro*, and a dab of guacamole.

POBLANO CREPES

CREPAS DE POBLANO

Yield: Serves 4 to 6

During the Maximilian Affair, in mid-nineteenth-century Mexico, the French and Mexicans came to blows. Afterward, one Gallic tradition that really caught on was crêpes. Locals simply adore them and you can find them on the streets, during festivals, and in restaurants.

1 cup all-purpose flour

2 large eggs

½ cup milk

⅜ cup cold water

¼ teaspoon salt

2 tablespoons unsalted butter, melted

1 *poblano* chile, roasted, peeled, and puréed

1. In a large mixing bowl, whisk together the flour and the eggs. Gradually add the milk and water, stirring to combine. Add the salt and butter and beat until smooth. Fold in the *poblano* purée.

2. Heat a lightly oiled griddle or skillet over medium-high heat. Using a 1-ounce ladle, pour the batter for each crêpe onto the griddle. Tilt the pan with a circular motion so that the batter coats the surface evenly. Cook for about 2 minutes, or until the bottom is light brown. Loosen with a spatula, turn, and cook the other side for the same amount of time.

BE CREATIVE

THESE POBLANO-FLAVORED CRÊPES ARE DELICIOUS FILLED WITH SCRAMBLED EGGS, OR DRESS THEM UP WITH SAUTÉED LOBSTER AND CRAB FOR A NEW YEAR'S DAY BRUNCH. USE WHATEVER LEFTOVERS YOU HAVE AROUND.

DOS CAMINOS
MEXICAN STREET FOOD

BANANA PANCAKES

PANQUÉQUES DE PLÁTANO

Yield: Serves 3 to 4

2 cups all-purpose flour

3 tablespoons sugar

2 ½ teaspoons baking powder

½ teaspoon salt

¼ teaspoon ground cinnamon, preferably *canela* (Mexican cinnamon)

⅛ teaspoon ground ginger

2 very ripe bananas, mashed well

2 large eggs

2 to 2 ¼ cups buttermilk

2 tablespoons melted butter, plus butter or oil to grease a skillet or griddle

This is a good recipe for your whole family to enjoy. For grown-ups, you might top them with sliced bananas sautéed in a little butter and rum. Pancakes came to Mexico from the United States. They call them panqueques, pronounced pan-KAY-keys.

1. Sift the flour, sugar, baking powder, salt, cinnamon, and ginger together into a large bowl. In a separate bowl, whisk the bananas, eggs, and 2 cups of buttermilk together; add to flour mixture, stirring only until smooth. Stir in the melted butter. If the batter seems too thick to pour, add a little more buttermilk.

2. Brush a griddle or large skillet with a little butter or oil and heat over medium-high heat. Pour ¼ cup of batter for each pancake onto the griddle and cook until the surface is bubbly and lightly browned on the bottom; using a spatula, turn and brown the other side.

PUMPKIN PANCAKES WITH TOASTED PEPITAS AND SPICED CREMA

PANQUEQUES DE CALABAZA

Yield: Serves 3 to 4

1 ¼ cups all-purpose flour

1 tablespoons sugar

2 teaspoons baking powder

1 teaspoon ground cinnamon, preferably *canela* (Mexican cinnamon)

¾ teaspoon salt

¼ teaspoon ground cloves

⅛ teaspoon ground allspice

1 ⅓ cups whole milk

¾ cup canned pumpkin purée

4 large eggs

4 tablespoons (½ stick) unsalted butter, melted

1 teaspoon vanilla extract

Oil or clarified butter for cooking

Warm maple syrup

Toasted *Pepitas* (recipe follows)

Spiced *Crema* (recipe follows)

Mexicans love all kinds of squashes, including pumpkin. From earliest times, they have used not only the flesh and seeds (pepitas), but the dried shells as serving dishes and leaves to wrap foods like tamales. Pumpkins always remind me of El Día de los Muertos, or the Day of the Dead, one of the most important celebrations in Mexico.

1. Prepare the Toasted *Pepitas* and Spiced *Crema* (right).

2. Sift the dry ingredients into a large bowl. In a medium-size bowl, whisk the milk, pumpkin, eggs, melted butter, and vanilla to blend well. Add the pumpkin mixture to the dry ingredients; whisk just until smooth.

3. Brush a large nonstick skillet with oil or clarified butter and heat over medium heat. Pour the batter by ⅓ cupfuls into the skillet and cook until bubbles form on the surface of the pancakes and the bottoms are lightly browned, about 2 minutes per side. Using a spatula, turn and cook the second side until browned. Serve with warm maple syrup, Toasted *Pepitas*, and Spiced *Crema*.

> AFTER TRAVELING AROUND MEXICO FOR "SERIOUS" CULINARY STUDY, I FREQUENTLY GO TO VIPS, A DECADES-OLD RESTAURANT CHAIN THAT'S KIND OF LIKE OUR IHOP. THE HOMEY MENU, SERVED TWENTY-FOUR HOURS A DAY, IS PURE COMFORT FOOD AND THEIR PANQUEQUES ARE OUTSTANDING.

TOASTED *PEPITAS*

½ cup *pepitas*
2 teaspoons honey
Zest of 1 orange
1 teaspoon sugar
½ teaspoon salt

1. Preheat the oven or toaster oven to 325°F.

2. In a mixing bowl, stir together the *pepitas*, honey, and orange zest. Sprinkle on the sugar and salt and toss to coat. Spread on a flat pan and toast for 5 minutes, stir, and toast for another 5 minutes or until they are golden brown and crisp.

SPICED *CREMA*

2 cups heavy cream
1 teaspoon molasses
Pinch of salt

In an electric stand or using a handheld mixer, beat the cream, molasses, and salt into soft peaks.

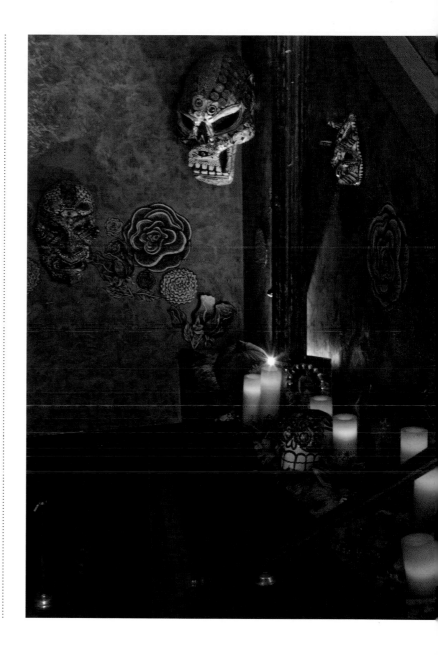

Day of the Dead Breakfast with Chef Carmen "Titita" Ramírez

My breakfast at El Bajío with Chef Carmen "Titita" Ramírez emphasized how cooking in Mexico—both at home and in restaurants—is a woman's domain. Titita, the matriarch-owner of this thirty-nine-year-old restaurant, is considered one of the world's best Mexican chefs; Ferran Adrià called her "the Queen of the Mexican kitchen." With the exception of a few "helpers," the kitchen was all women, and that's not uncommon. After dishes like *pipianada, carnitas*, and *chilaquiles negros*, we toured her colorful kitchen with its impressive collection of Day of the Dead artwork displayed.

In Mexico, El Día de los Muertos, or the Day of the Dead, is celebrated on November 1 and 2. The celebration dates back to early indigenous civilizations, including the Aztecs and Mayans, who commonly displayed skulls as ritualistic trophies symbolizing death and rebirth. After the Spanish conquered Mexico, Catholic priests moved the celebration to coincide with All Saints' Day (November 1) and All Souls' Day (November 2) on the Christian calendar. It is also a UNESCO-protected tradition.

While some cultures view death as macabre, Mexicans celebrate this passing as the beginning of yet another stage of life for their relatives, and they plan for the celebration throughout the year. From October 31 to November 2, families clean the graves and decorate them with offerings like a bottle of tequila or mezcal, colorful sugar skulls and candies, and *pan de muerto* (sweet egg bread made in different shapes, including those made to look like bones). Bright orange *cempasúchils* or marigolds, traditionally the *flor de muerto* (flower of death), are used because they are thought to attract the spirit of the dead. Offerings for dead children are frequently toys.

In well-to-do homes, families build altars or shrines that are decorated with pictures of departed relatives, candles, and a crucifix. Throughout Mexico, traditions vary vividly, but they are all characterized by the blend of traditional, pre-Hispanic Mexican, and Christian features.

ALMOND-STUFFED FRENCH TOAST WITH SOUR CHERRY SALSITA

PAN TORREJAS CON CEREZAS

Yield: Serves 6

Sour Cherry Salsita (recipe follows)

FILLING

½ pound mascarpone cheese

½ cup confectioners' sugar

1 teaspoon vanilla extract

½ teaspoon almond extract

¼ teaspoon salt

¼ cup almond milk (as needed)

FRENCH TOAST BATTER

8 large eggs

2 cups confectioners' sugar, plus sugar for dusting

½ cup heavy cream

½ cup almond milk

¼ cup whole milk

1 ½ teaspoons ground cinnamon, preferably *canela* (Mexican cinnamon)

1 ½ teaspoons ground ginger

12 (2-inch thick) slices brioche

2 cups sliced almonds

¾ cup clarified butter

Mint sprigs, for garnish

Maple syrup (optional)

Sweetened whipped cream (optional)

A Mexican breakfast is often a fiesta of flavors, colors, and textures. This indulgent French toast includes a tangy-sweet sour cherry salsita. I use the morita variety of dried jalapeños, known as morita chipotle chiles. The word means "little black-berry," referring to how the dark skin of the pepper looks. In Mexico, French toast is called Torrejas or Pan Frances. Use the delicious cherry salsa for crêpes or over the Coconut Ice Cream on page 232.

1. Prepare the Sour Cherry Salsita (at right).

2. Whip the mascarpone cheese and confectioners' sugar together until smooth; add the vanilla and almond extracts and salt. If needed, add some almond milk to thin the mixture to the consistency of thick cream. Refrigerate if not using right away.

3. In a large bowl, whisk the eggs, sugar, heavy cream, almond and whole milks, cinnamon, and ginger together; pour through a fine strainer into a shallow baking dish.

4. Cut a pocket in the side of each slice of brioche. Fill a pastry bag fitted with a plain tip with the filling and pipe about 2 tablespoons into each slice, pressing lightly to spread.

5. Soak the stuffed slices in the batter, taking care to cover both sides. Roll the soaked brioche slices in the sliced almonds, making sure all sides of the bread are crusted.

6. Heat a griddle or large skillet over medium-high heat and brush with clarified butter. Add only enough slices as will fit comfortably in the pan and cook until golden brown on one side, about 3 minutes; turn and cook the second side until golden, taking care not to burn the almonds.

7. Serve on a large oval platter or individual plates with a generous spoonful of Sour Cherry Salsita on top. Sprinkle with confectioners' sugar and garnish with a fresh mint sprig. Serve with maple syrup and sweet whipped cream, if desired.

SOUR CHERRY SALSITA

Yield: 3 ½ cups

1 *morita* chile, rehydrated and cut into strips
1 *ancho* chile, rehydrated and cut into strips
1 cup dried sour cherries
1 cup rosé wine
½ cup chopped *piloncillo* or firmly packed dark brown sugar
¼ cup freshly squeezed lime juice
½ cup bourbon
1 stick unsalted butter
1 cup frozen (or fresh, if available) sour cherries, halved and pitted
Salt

In a large saucepan, combine the *morita* and *ancho* chiles, dried cherries, *piloncillo*, lime juice, bourbon, and butter; cover and simmer for 15 minutes. Remove from the heat and let stand for 15 minutes. Scrape the sauce into a food processor and purée until smooth. Return the mixture to the saucepan, if necessary, to reduce the liquid to a syrupy consistency. Add the cherries and season to taste with salt.

VEGETABLES AND FRUITS
VEGETALES Y FRUTAS

GUACAMOLE

Yield: Serves 4

Dos Caminos' guacamole is probably our most famous dish. It's been voted the best in many different polls. We prepare it tableside in a lava stone molcajete according to each guest's specifications. The spice level can be raised or lowered by adjusting the amount of chile you add.

2 tablespoons finely chopped cilantro leaves

2 teaspoons finely chopped white onion

2 teaspoons minced *jalapeño* or *serrano* chiles, seeds and membranes removed if desired

½ teaspoon kosher salt

2 large ripe avocados, preferably Hass variety, peeled and seeded

2 tablespoons cored, seeded, and finely chopped plum tomatoes (about 1 small tomato)

2 teaspoons freshly squeezed lime juice

In a medium-size bowl or *molcajete*, use the back of a spoon to mash 1 tablespoon of the cilantro, 1 teaspoon onion, 1 teaspoon of minced chile, and ½ teaspoon salt together against the bottom of the bowl. Add the avocados and gently mash them with a fork until chunky-smooth. Fold the remaining cilantro, onion, and chile into the mixture. Stir in the tomatoes and lime juice, taste to adjust the seasonings, and serve with a basket of warm corn tortilla chips or *chicharrónes* (page 72).

GUACAMOLE IS AT ITS BEST WHEN MADE JUST BEFORE BEING SERVED. ANOTHER KEY TO SUCCESS IS CALIFORNIA-GROWN HASS AVOCADOS, BECAUSE THEY HAVE A CREAMIER, DENSER TEXTURE THAN ALL OTHER VARIETIES. WE SERVE THE DIP WITH WARM, HAND-CUT TORTILLA CHIPS. THIS RECIPE MAY BE MULTIPLIED AS MANY TIMES AS YOU LIKE. GENERALLY FIGURE THAT GUACAMOLE MADE WITH 1 AVOCADO SERVES 2 PEOPLE; 2 SERVES 4 TO 6; 3 AVOCADOS SERVES 6 TO 8.

GUACAMOLE WITH FRUIT
GUACAMOLE CON FRUTAS
Yield: Serves 2 to 4

1 ripe avocado, preferably Hass variety,
  peeled and seeded

½ tablespoon minced red onion

1 teaspoon minced *serrano* chile

12 red grapes, halved

¼ cup finely diced mango

¼ cup finely diced pineapple

Salt

Pomegranate seeds or halved blackberries,
  to garnish

Tortilla chips

My contemporary version of our beloved guacamole has a lot of fans, too.

Lightly mash the avocado, onion, and chile in a *molcajete*. Gently fold in the grapes, mango, and pineapple; season to taste with salt. Garnish with pomegranate seeds or blackberries and serve with chips.

FRIED PORK RINDS
CHICHARRÓNES
Yield: Serves 2 to 3

2 pounds pork rind or skin, with most of
  the fat trimmed and discarded

1 teaspoon salt

Vegetable oil, for frying

The ultimate crunchy snack to serve with guacamole! Sprinkle with chile powder after they are cooked, if you like a little heat.

1. Preheat the oven to 250°F.

2. Cut the pork rind into 2-inch squares, sprinkle with salt, and spread in a single layer on a jellyroll pan. Bake for 3 hours, drain the fat, and cool; store in a covered container until ready to use.

3. When ready to serve, pour enough oil into a large skillet to measure about 1 inch deep and heat until it measures 375°F on an instant-read thermometer. Fry the pork rinds until they puff up, 3 to 5 minutes. Drain and serve with guacamole.

JICAMA, ORANGE, AND APPLE SALAD

ENSALADA DE JICAMA, NARANJA Y MANZANA

Yield: Serves 6

1 medium jicama, peeled and cut into ¾-inch cubes

1 cup orange juice

1 teaspoon salt

1 tart apple, like Granny Smith, not peeled, cut into ¾-inch cubes

1 tablespoon freshly squeezed lemon juice

18 small romaine leaves

3 navel oranges, peeled and cut between the membranes into segments

1 ripe mango, peeled and cut into ¾-inch cubes

1 tablespoon julienned cilantro

1 teaspoon chile powder

Coarse sea salt

1 lime, quartered

This crunchy, tangy, and refreshing mixture is a fairly traditional Mexican salad found throughout the country. Jicama on its own has little taste, but it's the perfect crunchy carrier for a bright vinaigrette. Serve it as a side dish for sandwiches, omelets, or Sincronizadas (page 58).

1. In a bowl, combine the jicama, orange juice, and salt and refrigerate. In a separate bowl, cover the apples with water and add the lemon juice.

2. When ready to serve, line 6 plates with romaine leaves. Remove the jicama from the orange juice with a slotted spoon and reserve the juice. Combine the jicama with the oranges, apple, and mangos in a large bowl; add the cilantro and a couple of tablespoons of the reserved orange juice, and toss gently. Add a sprinkle of chile powder and coarse salt to taste; squeeze a lime wedge over each salad before serving.

 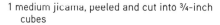

WARM CACTUS SALAD WITH PRICKLY PEAR VINAIGRETTE AND TOASTED PUMPKIN SEEDS

ENSALADA DE NOPALES CON VINAGRETA DE TUNAS Y PEPITAS

Yield: Serves 4

In this unique and appealing salad, a mixture of grilled cactus paddles with prickly pear and pumpkin seeds adds a fiesta of flavors and colors to your plates and palates. It highlights some indigenous ingredients of the desert.

2 *nopales* cactus paddles, cleaned

2 tablespoons vegetable oil

1 small red onion, cut into thin strips

1 tablespoon *pepitas* (pumpkin seeds), lightly toasted

¼ cup Prickly Pear Vinaigrette (recipe follows)

4 lime wedges

1. Preheat the grill or broiler. Put the paddles over the open grill or under the broiler and cook until just soft, about 2 minutes, turn once, and cook the second side for the same length of time. Set aside.

2. Heat the oil in a medium-size skillet over medium heat until hot. Add the onions and sauté until golden brown and caramelized. Set aside.

3. Slice cactus paddles and arrange on a platter. Spoon the onions on top and sprinkle on the *pepitas*.

4. Prepare the Prickly Pear Vinaigrette. Drizzle it over the cactus, squeeze on the lime juice, and add the squeezed wedges to the plate.

DOS CAMINOS
MEXICAN STREET FOOD

PRICKLY PEAR VINAIGRETTE

Yield: 2 cups

¼ cup red wine vinegar

1 tablespoon raspberry vinegar

½ teaspoon Dijon mustard

30 raspberries

¼ cup prickly pear syrup, available online or at Hispanic groceries

½ cup diced mango

Salt and freshly ground black pepper

Combine the vinegars, mustard, raspberries, and syrup in the jar of an electric blender and purée. Add the mango and purée until smooth. Strain the dressing into a bowl and season to taste with salt and pepper.

GRILLED NOPALES SALAD WITH CRACKED BLACK PEPPER OIL

NOPALES CON ACEITE DE PIMIENTA NEGRA

Yield: Serves 8

Grilled cactus paddles are a Mexican treat. Cooking them over charcoal adds a wonderful smoky flavor and firms up the texture. When tossed with red tomatoes, onions, green chiles, cucumbers, and white Cotija cheese, they make a festive summer dish for picnics and al fresco dining.

1 ½ pounds fresh *nopales* cactus paddles, needles removed (page 274)

¾ cup extra-virgin olive oil

1 ½ teaspoons salt

4 heirloom tomatoes, cut into ½-inch dice

2 cucumbers, peeled and cut into ½-inch dice

½ small red onion, cut into ¼-inch dice

2 medium *serrano* chiles, stemmed, seeded, and finely diced

1 cup chopped cilantro

½ cup *Cotija* cheese, finely grated

½ cup red wine vinegar

1 teaspoon dried oregano, preferably Mexican

1 teaspoon freshly ground black pepper

6 red lettuce leaves

1 avocado, preferably Hass variety, halved, peeled, seeded, and sliced, for garnish

Cracked Black Pepper Oil (recipe follows)

1. Heat a barbecue grill or broiler with the grill or pan positioned about 4 inches from the heat until hot.

2. In a bowl, toss the *nopales* with ¼ cup of the olive oil and ½ teaspoon of the salt; grill until marks appear on each side or they turn dark green with black patches, 2 to 3 minutes per side, turning once. Remove, cool to room temperature, cut into ½-inch pieces, cover, and chill for 2 to 4 hours, or overnight.

3. In a large bowl, combine the *nopales*, tomatoes, cucumbers, onion, chiles, cilantro, and cheese with the remaining ½ cup of oil, the vinegar, the oregano, the remaining teaspoon of salt, and the pepper. Toss well. Taste and adjust seasonings, as necessary.

4. Make the Cracked Black Pepper Oil and serve on plates lined with lettuce leaves, garnished with avocado slices, and drizzled with Cracked Black Pepper Oil.

CRACKED BLACK PEPPER OIL

Yield: ½ cup

¼ cup cracked black peppercorns
2 tablespoons extra-virgin olive oil
1 tablespoon red wine vinegar
1 teaspoon salt

In a small bowl, whisk together the peppercorns, olive oil, vinegar, and salt; stir before using.

DOS CAMINOS
MEXICAN STREET FOOD

STREET SALAD WITH HONEY-CITRUS-JALAPEÑO VINAIGRETTE

ENSALADA DE LA CALLE

Yield: Serves 6

Honey-Citrus-Jalapeño Vinaigrette
(recipe follows)

4 cups (about 6 ounces) baby romaine
lettuce

2 navel or other seedless oranges, peeled
and segmented

1 *each* small jicama, ripe mango, seedless
cucumber, and red papaya, peeled and cut
into 2 x ½ x ½-inch-thick pieces

½ ripe pineapple, peeled, cored, and cut into
2 x ½ x ½-inch-thick pieces

½ cup cilantro leaves

Classically, this Mexican street salad includes spears of fruits and vegetables served in a plastic cup or paper cone with a wedge of lime and a small packet of chile powder, and you eat it with your fingers. It's the perfect thing to eat when strolling around the zócalo, or central square in Mexico City. When entertaining at home, this is a more friendly way to eat it and you can prepare it a couple of hours ahead. The citrus vinaigrette can be used on any salad, like the one served with the Torta Desayuno on page 57.

1. Prepare Vinaigrette.

2. Put the romaine leaves on the bottom of a serving platter, drizzle with a little of the dressing, and toss. Spoon onto a serving platter or into 6 small bowls.

3. In a large mixing bowl, combine the oranges, jicama, mango, cucumber, papaya, and pineapple and gently toss with about ¼ to ½ cup of the vinaigrette. Spoon the jicama-fruit mixture over the romaine, sprinkle on the cilantro leaves, and serve the remaining dressing on the side.

HONEY-CITRUS-JALAPEÑO VINAIGRETTE

¼ cup red wine vinegar

¼ cup freshly squeezed orange juice

2 tablespoons freshly squeezed lime juice

2 tablespoons honey

1 tablespoon Dijon mustard

1 *jalapeño*, seeds and membranes removed, minced

½ cup olive oil

1 teaspoon salt

1 teaspoon freshly ground black pepper

In a bowl, vigorously whisk the vinegar, orange and lime juices, honey, mustard, *jalapeño*, oil, salt, and pepper together until mixed. It will be necessary to whisk again prior to using.

NEGRA MODELO BATTERED SQUASH BLOSSOMS STUFFED WITH REQUESÓN

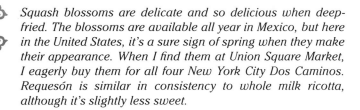

**FLORES DE CALABAZA FRITAS
RELLENO DE REQUESÓN**

Yield: Serves 4

Squash blossoms are delicate and so delicious when deep-fried. The blossoms are available all year in Mexico, but here in the United States, it's a sure sign of spring when they make their appearance. When I find them at Union Square Market, I eagerly buy them for all four New York City Dos Caminos. Requesón is similar in consistency to whole milk ricotta, although it's slightly less sweet.

BATTER

1 cup all-purpose flour

½ cup cornstarch

½ teaspoon salt

1 ½ cups Mexican beer, such as Negra Modelo

REQUESÓN-WILD MUSHROOM STUFFING

1 teaspoon vegetable oil, plus oil for frying

¼ cup finely chopped cremini mushrooms

2 garlic cloves, minced

½ cup *requesón* cheese or whole milk ricotta

2 tablespoons minced *epazote*

½ teaspoon *each* salt and pepper

16 large squash blossoms, washed

Salsa Verde (page 135)

1. Sift together the flour, cornstarch, and salt; stir in the beer until smooth. Cover and refrigerate for 30 minutes.

2. Meanwhile, prepare the stuffing. In a small skillet, heat the teaspoon of oil over medium-high heat. Add the cremini mushrooms and sauté until golden brown and the liquid has evaporated. Add the garlic, cook 30 seconds, and scrape into a bowl with the cheese, *epazote*, salt, and pepper and stir to blend.

3. Gently pull the leaves of each blossom to the side and remove the stamens. Open the blossoms and spoon a scant tablespoon of the stuffing mixture into the center of each. Avoid overfilling them. Gently twist the top of each blossom together to close. Place on a baking sheet and refrigerate for 15 minutes. Prepare the *Salsa Verde*.

4. Pour the oil into a large skillet to a depth of ½ inch. Heat over high heat to a temperature of 375°F on an instant-read thermometer or until a small cube of bread dropped into the oil turns golden brown within seconds.

5. Remove the batter from the refrigerator. Briefly dip each stuffed blossom into the batter, letting the excess batter fall back into the bowl, and carefully slide it into the hot oil. Cook until golden on all sides, about 3 minutes total cooking time. Add only as many blossoms as will fit comfortably in the skillet at one time. Transfer with a slotted spoon to paper towels to drain briefly.

6. Sprinkle with salt, if desired, and serve immediately with *Salsa Verde*.

 ALTHOUGH SQUASH BLOSSOMS ARE ALSO SOLD FROZEN OR CANNED, FOREGO THOSE AND SEEK THEM OUT IN SEASON IN YOUR GARDEN OR FARMERS' MARKETS AND YOU'LL BE REWARDED. REMEMBER TO REMOVE THE STAMENS AS THEY ARE BITTER.

DOS CAMINOS
MEXICAN STREET FOOD

ZUCCHINI WITH BLACK BEANS, PEPPERS, AND CHILES

CALABACITAS CON FRIJOLES NEGROS

Yield: Serves 6

2 tablespoons olive oil

3 cloves garlic, minced

1 large white onion, chopped

4 medium zucchini, diced

2 Thai chiles, seeds removed if desired, very thinly sliced

1 *poblano* chile, seeds removed if desired, diced

2 cups cooked or rinsed and drained canned black beans

1 cup corn kernels, fresh or frozen

1 tablespoon Maggi sauce (page 273)

Salt

Serve this colorful side dish with chicken, steak, or fish, or with the protein-rich Aztec grain quinoa as a delicious and healthful vegetarian entrée.

Heat the oil in a very large skillet over medium-high heat. Add the garlic and onion and cook until translucent, stirring frequently. Add the zucchini, Thai chiles, and *poblano* pepper and sauté until just tender but still slightly crisp, about 5 minutes. Stir in the black beans, corn, and Maggi sauce and heat through; season to taste with salt.

PICKLED RED CABBAGE

COL ROJA EN ESCABECHE

Yield: Serves 4 to 6

2 cloves garlic, thinly sliced

1 head red cabbage, cored and shaved

1 small red onion, thinly sliced lengthwise

1 *jalapeño*, seeds and membranes removed, thinly sliced lengthwise

Leaves from 2 sprigs oregano

2 cups apple cider vinegar

1 teaspoon sugar

Salt

Cabbage is frequently used in Mexican salads and as a condiment for tacos and other dishes. If you're a fan of Southern-style sweet and sour coleslaw, I think you'll love this.

Combine the garlic, cabbage, onion, *jalapeño*, and oregano in a large nonreactive bowl. Stir in the vinegar and sugar; season to taste with salt and let stand for at least 2 hours to overnight before serving.

MY REFRIED BEANS

MI FRIJOLES REFRITOS

Yield: Serves 6 to 8 generously
(about 2 quarts)

1 pound dry black or pinto beans

2 avocado leaves (page 272)

2 slices bacon, cut crosswise into ½-inch
  strips

1 small white onion, diced

2 cloves garlic, minced

2 *jalapeños*, seeds and membranes removed
  if desired, minced

½ cup lard

Juice of 1 lime

Salt

Crumbled *Cotija* cheese, to garnish (optional)

Lots of people have a favorite refried bean recipe, but I think my Dos Caminos version is special because we use avocado leaves and bacon, which adds a smoky flavor. They're definitely better than what comes out of a can. When we were very young children, one of the first foods my parents ordered for my sister and me were black bean tacos in a small storefront Mexican restaurant in Denver, where we ate weekly. They are a simple, approachable food for any age.

1. Rinse the beans and soak overnight in a large pot of cold water. (If you don't have time to soak overnight, put the beans into a pot of water to cover by at least 2 inches and bring to a boil; turn off the heat, cover, and let sit for 1 hour.) The following day, bring the pot of beans to a boil, add the avocado leaves, turn the heat down, and simmer until tender, 2 to 3 hours.

2. In a large skillet, cook the bacon over medium-high heat until golden brown; add the onion and sauté until golden, about 10 minutes. Stir in the garlic and *jalapeños* and cook for about 3 minutes, adding a little lard or bacon fat, if necessary, to keep the beans from sticking.

3. Drain the beans; reserve the cooking liquid. Scrape the onion mixture into the container of a food processor along with about 2 cups of the cooked beans and purée. Combine the purée with the remaining the beans.

4. In a large, heavy casserole, melt the lard over medium-high heat; add the beans and fry for about 15 minutes, stirring frequently. Add the lime juice and season to taste with salt. If the mixture seems dry, add some leftover bean water until you reach the desired consistency. Serve topped with crumbled *Cotija* cheese, if desired.

DRUNKEN BEANS

FRIJOLES BORRACHOS

Yield: Serves 6

1 pound pinto beans, soaked and cooked according to My Refried Beans (page 86)

4 quarts water

1 pound thin-sliced bacon, cut crosswise into ½-inch pieces

2 carrots, finely diced

2 cloves garlic, minced

1 white onion, finely diced

1 stalk celery, finely diced

6 sprigs thyme, stemmed and finely chopped

1 bunch fresh oregano, stemmed and finely chopped

1 tablespoon Dijon mustard

½ cup tomato paste

½ teaspoon ground allspice

1 canned *chipotle en adobo*, minced

2 (12-ounce) cans Mexican beer, preferably Tecate or Negra Modelo

Salt

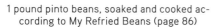

These beans are My Refried Beans dressed up with additional bacon, chipotles en adobo, mustard, and beer, which gives them the name borrachos, meaning "drunk." They're a perfect side dish for a Mexican-themed barbecue with grilled steak or chicken and Elote de la Calle (page 103).

Cook the bacon in a large casserole until done but not too crispy. Add the carrots, cloves, onion, celery, thyme, oregano, mustard, tomato paste, allspice, and chipotle and sauté until the vegetables are tender; stir in the beer, add the cooked beans to the pot, and simmer for 10 minutes to combine the flavors; season to taste with salt.

MASA AND BLACK BEAN CAKES WITH SPICY BUTTERNUT SQUASH

BOCOLES

Yield: Serves 6 as an entrée or 12 as an appetizer (*antojito*)

2 cups *Mole Coloradito* (page 32), heated

2 cups My Refried Beans (page 86)

2 tablespoons vegetable oil, plus oil for frying

4 cloves garlic, minced

1 white onion, diced

2 medium butternut squash, peeled and cut into 1-inch cubes (about 4 cups)

3 *jalapeños*, seeds and membranes removed, if desired, minced

1 teaspoon cumin powder

Salt

MASA

2 pounds (about 4 cups) *masa harina*

1 cup lard

½ cup chicken or vegetable stock, or more as needed

1 tablespoons salt

2 teaspoons baking powder

½ pound soft goat cheese, crumbled

Traditionally, bocoles are made with cornmeal mixed with lard and stuffed with marinated meat, potatoes, pork, etc. However, this version is ideal for vegetarians and anyone looking for a satisfying dish that is also gluten-free. In Oaxaca, they are commonly made with blue cornmeal and we do that in the restaurant. I love the nutty, corn flavor set against the soft, hot interiors. Both the mole sauce and refried beans may be made days ahead.

GARNISHES

Watercress sprigs

Julienned jicama

Spiced *Crema* (page 63)

Toasted *Pepitas* (page 63)

1. Prepare the *Mole Coloradito* and My Refried Beans.

2. Heat 2 tablespoons oil in a large skillet over medium heat. Add the garlic and onion and sauté for 1 minute. Add the butternut squash, *jalapeño*, cumin, and ½ teaspoon salt. Cook, stirring occasionally, until the squash is completely tender, 10 to 15 minutes; season to taste with salt.

3. Meanwhile, prepare the *masa*. In the bowl of a stand mixer, combine the *masa harina* and lard and beat until light. Add the stock and salt and beat until you have a smooth dough. Add the refried beans, baking powder, and 1 teaspoon of salt and mix until well blended. Add more salt, if needed. Roll golf ball–sized balls of dough, making a well in each with your thumb; fill each with a tablespoon of squash and a teaspoon of goat cheese.

4. Pat the balls between your hands into a pancake about ¼ inch thick and 2 inches in diameter. Wipe out the skillet, and add enough oil to the skillet to measure 1 inch deep; heat over medium-high heat to a temperature of 375°F on an instant-read thermometer. Fry the cakes until brown on the outside and cooked but still soft on the inside, about 3 or 4 minutes, turning once.

5. On individual taco plates, serve 3 *bocoles* over *Mole Coloradito*, topped with watercress sprigs and jicama. Drizzle with Spiced *Crema* and sprinkle with Toasted *Pepitas*.

STUFFED PLANTAIN CROQUETTES

CROQUETAS DE PLÁTANOS RELLENOS

Yield: 16 croquettes

1 cup My Refried Beans (page 86) or crumbled *queso fresco*

4 very ripe unpeeled plantains, cut in half lengthwise

4 tablespoons unbleached all-purpose flour

Salt

Vegetable oil, for frying

AS FOR *MASA*, THE WORD MEANS "DOUGH," AND YOU GENERALLY WANT A DRY, SORT OF PLAY-DOUGH TEXTURE THAT DOESN'T STICK TO YOUR FINGERS. ON THE STREETS, *CROQUETAS* ARE SERVED IN A PAPER CONE OR IN A BASKET LINED WITH A PAPER NAPKIN AND EATEN WITH BOTTLED HOT SAUCE.

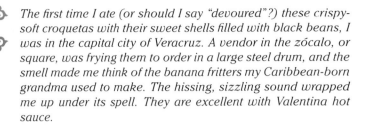

The first time I ate (or should I say "devoured"?) these crispy-soft croquetas with their sweet shells filled with black beans, I was in the capital city of Veracruz. A vendor in the zócalo, or square, was frying them to order in a large steel drum, and the smell made me think of the banana fritters my Caribbean-born grandma used to make. The hissing, sizzling sound wrapped me up under its spell. They are excellent with Valentina hot sauce.

1. Prepare My Refried Beans, if using. Preheat the oven to 350°F.

2. Roast the plantains on a sheet pan cut side up until the skins are black and the flesh is very soft and oozing, about 30 minutes. Cool, peel, and mash until smooth. Add the flour and salt to taste and mix well to form a smooth, dry *masa*.

3. With wet hands, form the dough into 2-inch balls. Make an indentation with your thumb in the center and fill with about 1 tablespoon of refried beans or cheese. Pat into patties about ½ inch thick and about 3 inches in diameter.

4. Pour enough oil into a 10-inch skillet to measure 1 inch deep and heat over medium-high heat until the oil registers 375°F on an instant-read thermometer. Lightly dust the *croquetas* with flour and add them a few at a time to the oil; fry until golden brown on both sides, turning once, about 3 minutes per side.

Sylvia Kurczyn's Chile Lesson

After breakfast in the hotel, we went to El Centro Culinario Ambrosía, Mexico City's equivalent to the Culinary Institute of America. The school trains professional chefs in its excellent facility and has a student-run restaurant.

My first class was an in-depth review of chiles with Sylvia Kurczyn, a robust woman with a thick braid cascading down her back and a starched white chef's jacket. Through a translator, Señora Sylvia discussed the characteristics of dried and fresh chiles in a unique way: she showed how to use all five of our senses in analyzing chiles and also in making taste comparisons, in much the way wine is analyzed. Of the 248 varieties of chiles used in Mexican cooking, 24 were displayed here. She made the point that chiles are not just used for heat; they also vary in flavors, so cooks can control how hot a dish is by understanding where each chile appears on the Scoville scale, the standard judge of heat. Cooks should become accustomed to tasting to determine how hot they want their dishes. This way of defining chiles would later be very helpful to me when teaching cooking classes and conducting server training.

We then continued on to making salsas, including *salsa borracha*, *x-ni-pek*, *chil-tomate*, and *salsa cruda de chile manzano*. Some of these were new to me and very interesting. After the salsa making, we proceeded to work on *chiles rellenos*, with some great recipes including a great *chile meco* stuffed with plaintain filling that I would later run as a special at Dos Caminos. After lunch we finished up by preparing adobos and aguas frescas. Dinner was at the Catalan restaurant Rac in the Condesa, where we had *butifara negra* (blood sausage) and red snapper *fideos*. Dessert was homemade *requesón* cheese with honey and chestnut ice cream with wine-soaked prunes.

DOS CAMINOS
MEXICAN STREET FOOD

VEGETARIAN EMPANADAS WITH CHILES AND CHEESE

EMPANADAS POTOSINAS

Yield: Serves 4 to 6

¼ cup cilantro leaves

1 recipe *Masa* (page 14)

Tomatillo-*Pasilla de Oaxaca* Salsa (page 21)

1 tablespoon vegetable oil, plus oil for frying

2 cloves garlic, minced

1 small white onion, finely chopped

2 *poblano* chiles, roasted, peeled, seeded, and julienned

1 *jalapeño*, seeded and minced

1 red bell pepper, roasted, peeled, seeds and membranes removed, and cut into strips

1 yellow bell pepper, roasted, peeled, seeds and membranes removed, and cut into strips

4 ounces *requesón* or ricotta

1 ounces *queso Chihuahua*

1 red potato, peeled, cut into ¼-inch cubes, and fried until golden

2 tablespoons julienned *epazote*

2 *costeño* chiles, toasted and crumbled

Salt

2 tablespoons crumbled *Cotija* cheese, for garnish

2 tablespoons *crema*, for garnish

Creamy, slightly spicy vegetarian empanadas like these are a popular regional snack in Central Mexico. The dough is bright green because the cilantro used to make the masa is blanched to set the color. Throughout Mexico, vegetarian food is common because meat can be expensive. These empanadas are among my favorite things to eat at Dos Caminos.

1. Blanch the cilantro in boiling water for 30 seconds, shock it in cold water, squeeze dry, and mince. You should have about 2 tablespoons. Prepare the *masa* according to the recipe, mix in the cilantro, roll the *masa* into 15 balls, and set aside. Prepare the Tomatillo-*Pasilla de Oaxaca* Salsa.

2. Heat 2 tablespoons of oil in a large skillet over medium-high heat until hot; add the garlic, onion, *poblano* and *jalapeño* chiles, and red and yellow peppers and sauté until limp; let cool to room temperature. Transfer to a large bowl, stir in the *requesón* and *Chihuahua* cheeses, potato, 1 tablespoon of the *epazote*, and *costeño* chiles; season to taste with salt.

3. Using a tortilla press, press the *masa* balls into 3-inch circles. Put 2 tablespoons of filling on one side of each empanada, fold in half, and press the edges to seal.

4. Add enough oil to a large skillet to measure 1 inch deep. Heat the oil over medium-high heat until hot or it registers 375°F on an instant-read thermometer. For each serving, fry 3 empanadas until golden on both sides, turning once. Remove and blot on paper towels. The empanadas may be kept briefly in a warm oven.

5. Spoon ¼ cup of Tomatillo-*Pasilla de Oaxaca* Salsa in the center of each taco plate and place the empanadas on top. Sprinkle with *Cotija* cheese, *crema*, and remaining *epazote* and serve.

TAMALES WITH HUITLACOCHE
TAMALES DE HUITLACOCHE

Yield: Serves 6

Huitlacoche, the famed corn fungus of Mexico, adds a mystical flavor to these tamales. There are whole cults of people devoted to it. You can buy it online either frozen or in cans (see "Resources"). Tamales often have nothing in the center beyond flavored masa, like these. For a vegetarian version, use solid vegetable shortening and vegetable stock.

1 pound dried cornhusks

1 cup *masa harina*

¾ cup warm water

½ cup chicken stock or vegetable stock

1 teaspoon salt

½ cup lard or solid vegetable shortening

2 cups canned or frozen *huitlacoche*, plus ½ cup for the *huitlacoche crema* (page 273)

½ cup coarsely chopped cilantro

½ cup crumbed *Cotija* cheese

Julienned radishes, for garnish

1. In a bowl, cover the cornhusks with warm water and soak until pliable, about 30 minutes.

2. For the tamales, moisten the *masa harina* with the water, chicken stock, and salt; set aside. In a stand mixer fitted with a paddle attachment, beat the lard or shortening until creamy and fluffy, about 20 minutes. Stir in the *masa* mixed with the water and chicken stock, mix well, and set aside.

3. In the jar of an electric blender, purée the *huitlacoche* and cilantro with a little water until smooth. Scrape this mixture into the dough and blend well. Adjust the seasoning with salt and pepper.

4. To assemble the tamales, open the cornhusks and place 1 tablespoon of dough in the center of the cornhusk. Fold over the sides of the cornhusk, roll up, and tie the ends with a piece of string. Repeat the process until all the dough is used.

5. In a double boiler with a steamer insert, bring the water to a boil; add the tamales, cover, and steam 40 to 45 minutes until done. Test by opening one tamale; if it releases easily, the tamales are done. Do not overcook.

6. While the tamales are steaming, combine the remaining *huitlacoche* and *crema*.

7. Remove the tamales from the steamer and allow them to sit for 5 minutes. Then open them and serve with a sprinkle of cheese, a generous teaspoonful of *huitlacoche crema*, and julienned radish.

DIFFERENT WAYS TO ROLL TAMALES

TAMALES CAN BE ROLLED AND TIED IN SEVERAL WAYS. THE MOST BASIC WAYS ARE SECURED AT BOTH ENDS LIKE A TOOTSIE ROLL, BUNDLED AND TIED LIKE A PACKAGE, OR SIMPLY FOLDED LIKE AN ENVELOPE.

TAMALES (STEP BY STEP)

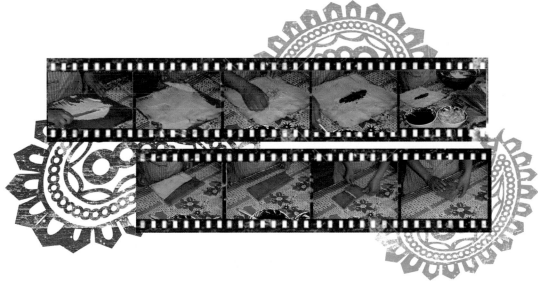

CORN-STUFFED CHILES

ANCHO CHILES RELLENOS DE ELOTE CON CREMA

Yield: Serves 4 to 6 (15 chiles)

In this tasty dish, ancho chile peppers, rehydrated in tangy-sweet piloncillo-sherry vinegar water, are filled with creamy corn and baked.

2 cups water

1 cup sherry vinegar

½ cup chopped *piloncillo*

1 tablespoon salt

20 medium *ancho* chiles

Creamed Corn (recipe follows)

1 (16-ounce) bag baby spinach leaves, washed and spun dry

3 red onions, sliced in ½-inch-thick rounds, grilled or broiled until black on each side, turning once

Juice of ½ lime

1. Line a sheet pan with parchment paper. Preheat the oven to 350°F. Lightly oil a baking dish.

2. Combine the water, vinegar, *piloncillo*, and salt in a medium-size saucepan and bring to a boil; reduce the heat and simmer until the sugar is melted, about 2 minutes.

3. Toast the chiles and put them in a nonreactive bowl. Pour on the *piloncillo*-sherry mixture and soak until rehydrated, 20 to 30 minutes; remove from the liquid, make a slit from stem to tip in each chile, and remove the seeds and veins. Any discards from the chiles should be chopped and folded in with the filling. Lay the chiles on the sheet pan and cover with a damp towel. Reduce the soaking liquid over medium-low heat into a syrup, 15 to 20 minutes; strain and reserve.

4. Prepare the Creamed Corn.

5. Fill the chiles with the creamed corn mixture, lay them in the baking dish, transfer to the oven, and heat until warmed through, about 15 minutes.

6. To serve: toss the spinach and charred onions with a little of the reserved sherry-*piloncillo* syrup mixed with the lime juice; serve on individual plates. Place the hot chiles on top of the salad, pushed open slightly like a baked potato, and sprinkle with cilantro. Drizzle the sherry-*piloncillo* reduction over the plate and serve.

ALTHOUGH YOU START WITH 20 CHILES, NOT ALL WILL SURVIVE. USE ANY BROKEN PIECES TO SEASON THE FILLING. IF YOU LIKE *CHILES RELLENOS*, SEE THE RECIPES FOR THOSE FILLED WITH CHICKEN OR WITH TURKEY PICADILLO (PAGE 156 AND 162). IF YOU HAVE A LITTLE EXTRA FILLING, SERVE AS A SIDE DISH TO ANY GRILLED MEAT OR POULTRY.

 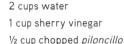

CREAMED CORN

Yield: 3 quarts

2 pounds corn kernels, divided

½ cup chicken stock

1 cup heavy cream, divided

2 tablespoons unsalted butter

2 white onions, diced

2 tablespoons minced garlic

½ pound roasted *poblano* chiles, seeded and diced

Salt and freshly ground black pepper

¼ cup chopped cilantro, plus julienned cilantro to garnish

1. In a medium saucepan, combine 1 pound of corn, the chicken stock, and ⅓ cup of the cream and heat over medium-high heat for 1 minute; scrape the mixture into the container of a food processor, add the remaining ⅔ cup cream, and purée until smooth.

2. Melt the butter in a large saucepan over medium heat. Stir in the onions and sauté until soft; add the garlic and cook 1 minute more. Add the remaining pound of corn, the *poblanos*, and any leftover *ancho* chiles, and heat gently.

3. Stir the puréed mixture into corn-*poblano* mixture, lower the heat, and simmer for about 10 minutes, stirring occasionally to avoid sticking and burning. Season to taste with salt and pepper; add the cilantro and keep warm.

PLANTAIN-STUFFED CHIPOTLE CHILES

CHIPOTLES CHILES RELLENOS DE PLÁTANO

Yield: Serves 6 as an *antojito* (appetizer)

30 *chipotle morita* chiles

½ (6-ounce) cone *piloncillo*, plus 2 tablespoons grated

¼ cup vegetable oil, plus more for frying

1 small red onion, finely chopped

1 clove garlic, minced

3 plum tomatoes, peeled, seeded, and diced

1 teaspoon dried oregano, preferably Mexican

2 ripe plantains, peeled and finely diced

5 ounces soft goat cheese

All-purpose flour seasoned with salt and pepper, for dredging

6 large eggs, separated

Green salad, if desired

1. Put the *chipotle moritas* in a large bowl. Fill a 4-quart saucepan halfway with water, bring to a simmer, add the ½ cone of *piloncillo*, and cook until dissolved. Carefully pour enough of the sweetened hot water over the chiles to cover, put a plate on top of the chiles so they remain submerged, and soak for 20 minutes. Drain and gently pat dry with paper towels.

I learned to make these tasty little chiles stuffed with plantains and goat cheese about a year ago in Mexico City at El Centro Culinario Ambrosía, the country's top culinary school (see sidebar on page 208). At Dos Caminos we serve them topped with a frisée, watercress, and shaved radicchio salad tossed with sliced radishes and vinaigrette made with the piloncillo syrup on page 274, mixed with lime juice and olive oil. You might also serve the salad on page 81.

2. With a small, sharp knife, make a 1-inch lengthwise slit in each chile without cutting all the way through. Using a demitasse spoon, carefully remove the seeds and membranes.

3. In a medium-size saucepan, heat the oil over medium heat. Add the onion and sauté until soft and translucent. Add the garlic and cook until it just begins to brown. Stir in the tomatoes and oregano and cook for about 15 minutes over low heat to blend the flavors, adjusting the salt as necessary.

4. Add the plantain and gently mash with the back of a spoon to form a textured paste. Remove from heat and stir in the 2 tablespoons grated *piloncillo* and goat cheese until combined.

5. Stuff each chile with about 1 ½ teaspoons of the mixture and fold the edges of the slit together to seal.

6. Pour enough oil into a large skillet to measure 1 inch; heat over medium-high heat until the oil measures 375°F on an instant-read thermometer.

7. Meanwhile, in a stand mixer or using a handheld mixer, whip the egg whites into stiff peaks. Slowly add the yolks, one at a time. Just prior to frying, dip each chile in the flour and then in the egg mixture. Add them to the skillet, a few at a time, and fry until golden brown, turning once; remove to paper towels to drain.

8. Serve 3 chiles topped with a small green salad.

MASHED CARIBBEAN SWEET POTATOES WITH GARLIC

PURÉ DE BONIATO CON MOJO

Yield: Serves 4

White Caribbean sweet potatoes, or boniato, are commonly used in Mexico but they aren't always readily available in the United States. You can substitute yams, American sweet potatoes, or butternut squash for this tangy side dish.

1 ½ pounds *boniato* (3 to 4), yams, sweet potatoes, or butternut squash, peeled and cut into medium-size cubes

Milk, to cover

1 tablespoon vegetable oil

¼ cup thinly sliced garlic

Juice of 2 to 3 limes

Salt and freshly ground black pepper

1. In a large saucepan, cover the *boniato* with milk and cook over low heat until tender, 30 to 40 minutes.

2. Meanwhile, heat the oil in a small skillet over medium-high heat until hot. Stir in the garlic and cook until golden brown, shaking the pan often; add the lime juice and season to taste with salt and pepper.

3. Drain the *boniato* and, while hot, pass it through a food mill or mash with a potato masher. Add the garlic mixture and taste to adjust the salt and pepper.

DOS CAMINOS
MEXICAN STREET FOOD

MEXICO CITY–STYLE STREET CORN

ELOTE DE LA CALLE

Yield: Serves 8

8 ears corn, shucked

½ cup melted unsalted butter

½ cup mayonnaise

½ cup grated *Cotija* cheese

1 tablespoon chile powder

2 limes, cut into wedges

 DOS CAMINOS STYLE

AT DOS CAMINOS, THE
CORNHUSKS ARE SERVED
FETCHINGLY BRAIDED, MUCH
TO DINERS' DELIGHT.

Everybody loves corn like they serve it in Mexico City. Almost anywhere in the center of town, or near most markets, you can smell the seductive aroma of charred cornhusks coming from vendor carts. No matter where you're from or who you are, the grilled sweet corn painted with butter and a little mayonnaise and salty Cotija cheese will seduce you.

Heat the grill, a large skillet, or a broiler over medium-high heat. Grill the corn until hot and lightly charred all over, using tongs to turn it. Roll the ears in the melted butter and then spread with mayonnaise. Sprinkle with *Cotija* cheese and chile powder and serve with lime wedges.

PAN-FRIED STREET CORN
ESQUITES DE LA CALLE

Yield: Serves 8

Pan-fried kernels of corn with crème fraîche, Cotija cheese, and epazote is an addictive way that you, like Mexicans, can enjoy seasonal corn served in a plastic cup from a vendor's cart.

16 large ears corn, shucked

½ cup *crème fraîche* or sour cream or *crema*

4 tablespoons unsalted butter

2 large shallots, finely chopped

2 *poblano* chiles, seeded and diced

2 cups water

½ cup crumbled *Cotija* cheese, plus 2 table-spoons to garnish

3 tablespoons thinly sliced *epazote*, plus 1 tablespoon to garnish

Salt and freshly ground black pepper

1. Using a sharp paring knife, cut the kernels from cobs and set aside. Scrape the dull side of the blade several times against the cobs to extract the remaining corn pulp, scraping it into a large glass measuring cup. (You should have at least 1 ½ cups of corn pulp. If not, add enough *crème fraîche* to measure 1 ½ cups.) Transfer the pulp to the jar of an electric blender and purée until smooth.

2. Heat the butter in a shallow medium-size saucepan over medium heat. Add the shallots and peppers and cook until softened, 3 to 4 minutes, stirring occasionally. Add the corn kernels, corn purée, water, *Cotija* cheese, *epazote*, and salt and pepper to taste; simmer uncovered until the kernels are just tender, 3 to 4 minutes, stirring occasionally. Serve garnished with the remaining *epazote* and *Cotija* cheese.

SAFFRON TOASTED PASTA

SAFFRON FIDEOS

Yield: Serves 4 to 6

1 pound *fideos* or other dried vermicelli-like noodle

2 cups heavy cream

1 tablespoon dried saffron

Salt

⅓ cup olive oil

8 cloves garlic, sliced

This is really neither a vegetable nor fruit, but fideos are as old as the hills in Mexico and arguably every kid's favorite comfort food. I updated and enriched the dish with saffron and cream and gave it a tempting, crispy topping by broiling it at the end. It lends itself to adding vegetables, just as you might to pasta primavera.

1. Heat the oven to 375°F.

2. Arrange the *fideos* in an even layer on a jellyroll pan and toast until golden brown; remove and set aside to cool.

3. Turn on the broiler.

4. In a small saucepan, combine the cream, saffron, and 1 teaspoon of salt; whisk to dissolve the saffron. Bring to a boil over high heat, remove from heat, and let cool.

5. In a medium-size skillet, heat the oil and garlic over low heat until the garlic begins to soften. Add the cream mixture and reduce by one third, add the *fideos*, and cook for 3 minutes. Return the mixture to the jellyroll pan and broil until golden brown.

SPINACH WITH PUMPKIN SEEDS AND RAISINS

ESPINACAS CON PEPITAS Y PASAS

Yield: Serves 4

2 ½ pounds baby spinach, stemmed

2 to 3 tablespoons olive oil

2 small white onions or 6 green onions, minced

4 tablespoons raisins, plumped in hot water and drained

¼ cup *pepitas*, lightly toasted

Salt and freshly ground pepper

Toasted pumpkin seeds and raisins transform ho-hum spinach to an unexpected delight. It's my spin on the classic Galician spinach dish espinacas a la gallegas made with pine nuts and currants.

1. Rinse the spinach well and shake to remove most of the water. Put it in a large skillet and cook over medium heat until wilted, a few minutes, turning as needed. Drain well and set aside.

2. Add the olive oil to the empty pan and return to medium heat. Add the onions and sauté until tender, about 8 minutes. Add the spinach, raisins, and *pepitas* and sauté briefly to warm through; season with salt and pepper to taste and serve warm or at room temperature.

Ceviches

The new "in" food of the beginning of the twenty-first century is actually an Old World dish from South America called *ceviche*. It has been one of Latin America's best-kept secrets for centuries, but ceviche is becoming a popular appetizer and will continue to gain in popularity.

Ceviche's birthplace is disputed, and is either Peru or Ecuador. As both countries have an amazing variety of fish and shellfish, it could easily have come from the ancient Incan civilizations of Peru and Ecuador. Every Latin American country has given ceviche a touch of individuality by adding unique garnishes.

In Peru, ceviche is served with slices of cold sweet potatoes or corn on the cob. In Ecuador, it is accompanied by popcorn, potato chips, nuts, or corn nuts. It is also served in a large crystal bowl with guests helping themselves either by spearing pieces with toothpicks or filling pastry shells. In Mexico, ceviche is accompanied by slices of raw onions and served on toasted tortillas, and is considered their national dish.

Diana Nuñez de Smolij, a Peruvian food scholar now living in Ecuador, offers the following information on the history of ceviche:

There is a theory that pre-Hispanic peoples cooked fish with a fruit called *tumbo*. The Incas ate salted fish and fish marinated in *chicha*, a low-alcohol beer made from corn. The Spanish contributed the Mediterranean custom of using lemons and onions. Other historians believe ceviche's origin is the Arabian Peninsula and that it was brought to Peru by Arab immigrants and then reinterpreted by Peruvians of the coastal areas.

The other popular version told about its origins is that some English-speaking people who watched fishermen on the coast of Peru eating their fish directly from the sea with just lemons and salt said: "See the beach." Since this is a phrase that locals couldn't repeat well, they pronounced it "ceviche" instead.

Latin American flavors first found a place on Florida menus with South Florida's "New World Cuisine" in the late 1980s. This cuisine comes from the diverse cooking styles and tropical ingredients of the Caribbean, Latin America, and Central and South America. Florida's chefs became fascinated by the tempting flavors of exotic tropical fruits and vegetables. From this fascination, many versions of ceviche were developed.

The ceviches we serve at Dos Caminos are contemporary and international in style but draw on classic ingredients, techniques, and flavor combinations.

Our lobster ceviche is prepared with poached Maine lobster, *habanero*-infused coconut milk, mango, mint, and cilantro and is served in its shell.

Tuna ceviche is a "Chino-Latino" style ceviche that is very popular in South America, whose culinary style is influenced by the large Asian population. It combines sushi-grade tuna with spicy seaweed, soy-lime marinade, toasted sesame seeds, and *chiles torreados*. *Chiles torreados* are a classic Mexican condiment made with *jalapeños* or *serrano* chiles sautéed with onion and garlic and marinated in lime and Maggi, Mexican steak and seafood sauce (page 273).

Shrimp ceviche is made from jumbo white shrimp lightly tossed in a Veracruz-style *cascabel* chile and passionfruit marinade. It is served in a chilled bowl topped with scallions, avocado, and toasted garlic chips.

PISMO CLAM CEVICHE WITH TABASCO RASPADO

CEVICHE DE ALMEJAS

Yield: Serves 2 (may be doubled)

While studying history at UCLA, I often drove down the coast to Ensenada, in Baja California. There I discovered the large (they can be up to 7 inches long), juicy, and sweet Pismo clams that are exclusive to the California and Mexican coast. I'd eat them raw and in ceviches, at the mariscos or shellfish stand, where "La Guerrerense" (the Woman from Guerrero, named Sabina Bandera Gonzalez) is probably world famous at this point for the amazing freshness and quality of her mariscos, or shellfish. Pismos were always my favorite. As its name suggests, Tabasco Raspado is quite spicy.

8 Pismo clams

2 tablespoons Tabasco Raspado (recipe follows)

Crushed ice

Lime wedges, for garnish

Maldon or other coarse sea salt, for garnish

Cilantro leaves, for garnish

1. Prepare the Tabasco Raspado.

2. Shuck the clams and free the muscle from the shell, reserving the clam juice for Tabasco Raspado or other recipes, if desired.

3. Line a shallow bowl with crushed ice. Arrange the clams on the half shell on the ice. Top each with a squeeze of lime, a sprinkle of salt, and a shaving of the Tabasco Raspado. Top with a cilantro leaf and serve with a wedge of lime.

TABASCO RASPADO

Yield: 1 cup

½ cup tomato juice, chilled until very cold

¼ cup freshly squeezed lime juice

¼ cup Tabasco sauce, chilled until very cold

2 tablespoons bottled clam juice (or reserved liquor from previously shucked clams), chilled until very cold

Salt

In a bowl, combine the tomato juice, lime juice, Tabasco sauce, and bottled clam juice; season to taste with salt. Pour the mixture into a shallow square glass or metal dish and transfer to the freezer, scraping the mixture with a fork every 20 minutes until frozen, about 2 to 3 hours. When frozen, scrape across the surface with a fork to serve.

 CEVICHE, WHICH IS OFTEN SPELLED "SEVICHE" OR "CEBICHE" DEPENDING ON WHICH PART OF LATIN AMERICA IT COMES FROM, IS SEAFOOD PREPARED IN A CENTURIES-OLD METHOD OF COOKING BY CONTACT WITH THE ACID OF CITRUS JUICE INSTEAD OF HEAT. IT CAN BE EATEN AS A FIRST COURSE OR MAIN DISH, DEPENDING ON WHAT IS SERVED WITH IT. THE PREPARATION AND CONSUMPTION OF CEVICHE IS PRACTICALLY A RELIGION IN PARTS OF MEXICO AND CENTRAL AND SOUTH AMERICA, AND IT SEEMS AS THOUGH THERE ARE AS MANY VARIETIES OF CEVICHE AS PEOPLE WHO EAT IT.

ISTHMIAN-STYLE SCALLOP CEVICHE

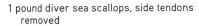

CEVICHE DE VENERAS A LA ISTMEÑO

Yield: Serves 2 to 4

I first tasted this scallop ceviche in the Isthmus of Tehuantepec, a fascinating place with a unique cuisine. It's one of the coolest places I have ever been to. Inspired, I prepared a dinner at the James Beard House that focused on this cuisine. The obvious secret to success for this dish is to use impeccably fresh "dry" scallops: those that haven't been soaked in phosphates or other preservatives to plump them up.

1 pound diver sea scallops, side tendons removed

1 cup freshly squeezed lime juice

2 tablespoons vegetable oil

Juice of *each* 1 lime, 1 orange, and 1 grapefruit

2 *habanero* chiles, seeded and thinly sliced

1 tablespoon thinly sliced scallion

1 tablespoon julienned cilantro leaves

1 ½ teaspoons grated fresh ginger

1 ½ teaspoons Maggi sauce (page 273)

1 teaspoon rice vinegar

Salt

Fresh seaweed, for garnish (optional)

Avocado slices, preferably Hass variety, for garnish (optional)

1. Cut the scallops crosswise into ⅛-inch-thick slices. Put them in a glass or porcelain bowl and pour the lime juice over them. Refrigerate for 30 minutes (don't marinate too long because it will toughen them), then remove from the marinade.

2. In a clean bowl, combine the scallops with the oil, citrus juices, chiles, scallion, cilantro, ginger, Maggi sauce, and vinegar and gently stir. Season to taste with salt and serve on a bed of fresh seaweed garnished with avocado slices.

Four Days in the Isthmus of Tehuantepec

The dramatic and startling Isthmus of Tehuantepec sits at the bottom of a steep, five thousand-foot descent down the Chiapas Depression. It's a land of almost constant heat and humidity. I found the inhabitants of this coastal plain, the istmeños, to be among Oaxaca's most unique and charismatic regional groups. And their imposing women have a remarkable demeanor: they really kick butt.

The Isthmus is barely a hundred miles wide with lush tropical lowlands watered by rivers that run down to the sea. It is bordered by the States of Chiapas, Veracruz, Tabasco, and Oaxaca. Before the Panama Canal, it was an important shipping point between the Gulf of Mexico and the Pacific Ocean, with a once-important railway connecting the two coasts.

Groves of mangos, oranges, almonds, and coconuts are virtually everywhere; and the local avocados along with those from Chiapas are among the largest and most flavorful grown in Mexico. The proximity of the isthmus to the sea is also vital to istmeños, offering huge quantities of fish and shellfish. Mullet, flounder, and shrimp are so plentiful that once local restaurants have bought their share of fresh fish most of the day's catch is either salted or smoked. The abundance of fish, fruit, and fertile farmland is reflected in the locals' lifestyle. They are known for their more than one hundred fiestas, called velas, celebrated each year in the barrios of the towns of Juchitan and Tehuantepec.

The istmeños society is matriarchal: women run the markets and those men who are not employed as farmers or fishermen stay home with the children and older people.

I was fascinated by this female dominance, which tends to be the case throughout Mexico. At barrio fiestas, for example, women dance with each other while the men sit on the sidelines, clearly knowing their place. The women are large and stately, and their everyday dress is only slightly less exotic than that worn at the *velas*. The sight of the embroidered *huipiles*, long *rabona* skirts, glistening gold jewelry, and floral hair adornments adds to the already exotic appearance of the Tehuantepec and Juchitan markets. As a chef, I was inspired because the women radiate quiet strength and men just don't mess with them—they mean business.

With such a profusion of culinary resources, the variety of foods in these markets is extensive. Wild animals, such as birds, iguanas, and armadillos used for tamales and stews are sold along with pigs and chickens, fish and shellfish. Huge piles of shrimp, especially in the Juchitan market, are ubiquitous. Shrimp not used immediately are boiled right in the seawater after being caught and then left to dry out. They are the basis for a variety of prepared foods sold in the markets, such as *caldos*, or soups, and *gueta bínguí*, their awesome light and airy shrimp croquettes.

Smoked mullet is also a popular prepared food, as are marinated and cooked chicken and pork. Local cheeses made with red and green *jalapeños* and cornbread made with ground fresh corn kernels and baked in large sardine tins are other local treats to be savored. The spices, especially the *achiote* pastes used in similar fashion in both chicken and pork marinades, were reminiscent of those I discovered in the markets in the Yucatán.

In Juchitan, every day is market day, with vendors filling the streets around the market with fresh produce. In Tehuantepec, *tianguis*—or street markets named for the Nahuatl word for "awning"—are held on Sundays and Wednesdays. Transport to the markets is by motocarro, a three-wheeled motorcycle with a small flatbed built on top of the rear wheels. The tehuana women riding in them make a memorable sight with their long skirts billowing out behind them on their way to the *tianguis*.

Finally, I visited some of the small beach communities that dot the Gulf of Tehuantepec, where city folk go to get away. Along the coast there are several small seafood restaurants featuring the catch of the day. Women with baskets of freshly caught fish balanced on their heads go from restaurant to restaurant vending their wares, which turn into the star attractions of the day's *comida*.

RED SNAPPER CEVICHE
CEVICHE DE HUACHINANGO

Yield: Serves 6

1 ½ cups red snapper Ceviche Marinade (recipe follows)

12 ounces red snapper fillet, thinly sliced crosswise

6 tablespoons finely diced tomato

2 tablespoons finely julienned cucumber

2 tablespoons thinly sliced red onion

1 tablespoon thinly sliced cilantro leaves

1 tablespoon finely julienned *jalapeño*

Salt

Small romaine spears, to garnish

Tortilla chips, to garnish

3 limes, thinly sliced

This traditional ceviche is all about the wonderfully sweet flavor of the fresh snapper combined with crunchy fresh vegetables. It's like those you find in almost any Mexican seaside village. Fishermen make the best ceviches right on the dock with their fresh catch.

1. Make the Ceviche Marinade (below).

2. Put the snapper in a small bowl, add the Ceviche Marinade, and toss to coat evenly. Add the tomato, cucumber, onion, cilantro, *jalapeños*, and salt to taste. Let stand for no more than 5 minutes to retain the snapper's freshness and texture.

3. Serve in an ice cream bowl garnished with spears of romaine, tortilla chips, and lime slices.

CEVICHE MARINADE

Yield: 1 ½ cups

½ cup bottled clam juice

⅓ cup freshly squeezed lime juice

3 tablespoons tomato juice

2 tablespoons freshly squeezed orange juice

2 tablespoons Valentina or other hot sauce

½ tablespoon extra-virgin olive oil

Salt and freshly ground black pepper

Combine the marinade ingredients in the jar of an electric blender and purée until smooth; season to taste with salt and pepper.

CAMPECHANA-STYLE SEAFOOD COCKTAIL

CAMPECHANA

Yield: Serves 4

Campechana-style cocktail sauce is a secret ingredient to enliven just about any fish or shellfish combination. In Ensenada, California, this flavorful, mildly spicy sauce is typically tossed with shellfish and diced avocado, and served in big parfait glasses with "Saladitas," or saltine crackers, on the side. They sell it at the stalls that line the fish markets. You'll need about half of the sauce for this recipe; the rest can be refrigerated for several weeks.

1 (14-ounce) bottle tomato ketchup

1 (8-ounce) bottle clam juice

1 (6-ounce) can tomato juice

Juice of 2 oranges

Juice of 1 grapefruit

¼ cup Worcestershire sauce

2 canned *chipotles en adobo*

2 stalks celery, coarsely chopped

1 large shallot, coarsely chopped

1 *jalapeño*, seeds and membranes removed

1 teaspoon Dijon mustard

1 tablespoon cilantro leaves

Salt and freshly ground black pepper

10 ounces mixed seafood, such as cooked diced shrimp or lobster, steamed mussels or clams out of their shells, and white fish

1 avocado, preferably Hass variety, peeled and diced

1. Combine the ketchup, clam juice, tomato juice, orange and grapefruit juices, Worcestershire, *chipotle*, celery, shallot, *jalapeño*, and mustard in the jar of an electric blender and purée until smooth. Pour into a bowl, fold in the cilantro, and season to taste with salt and pepper. Transfer to storage jars and refrigerate.

2. In a bowl, combine the seafood, avocado, and half of the salsa; gently stir to blend. Spoon into large parfait or other wide glasses and serve.

SHRIMP IN AGUACHILE

CAMARONES AGUACHILE

Yield: Serves 3 to 4

2 cups freshly squeezed lime juice

2 small cucumbers, peeled and seeded

4 *serrano* chiles, seeded

1 chicken bouillon cube

1 tablespoon chopped mint leaves

1 tablespoon chopped cilantro leaves

1 (500 mg) vitamin C tablet

12 large shrimp, poached and butterflied

½ cup thinly sliced red onions

½ cup julienned cucumber

½ cup julienned radish

2 tablespoons julienned mint leaves

2 tablespoons chopped cilantro leaves

In Mexico, I discovered they use a lot of curious ingredients in their cooking, like animal crackers, deviled ham, and the vitamin C tablets that turn this flavorful dish bright green. It's a lively, piquant way to enjoy fresh shrimp that's also colorful and crunchy. Sinaloa and Nayarit both claim that camarones aguachile originated there, and each of these coastal resorts has their own unique style. As a child, I ate the dish in Mazatlán and Puerta Vallarta (Nayarit), from which comes the version below.

1. In the jar of an electric blender, combine the lime juice, cucumbers, *serrano* chiles, bouillon cube, mint leaves, cilantro leaves, and vitamin C tablet; purée until very smooth and pour through a fine strainer.

2. To serve: ladle ¼ cup of the aguachile into 4 chilled wide soup bowls; lay the shrimp on top so that they are partially covered. Toss the cucumber, radish, mint, and cilantro in a little of the aguachile and spoon into the center of the shrimps.

COCONUT "RETURN TO LIFE" COCKTAIL

VUELVE LA VIDA DE COCO

Yield: Serves 4

½ pound large shrimp, shelled and deveined, shells reserved

1 tablespoon olive oil

1 clove garlic, finely chopped

Juice of 3 limes

½ pound sea scallops, side tendons removed

1 tablespoon finely diced red onion

1 coconut

1 bunch cilantro, coarse stems removed, rinsed, and blotted dry

1 tablespoon finely chopped mint

1 *jalapeño*, seeds and membranes removed, finely diced

½ avocado, preferably Hass variety

¼ teaspoon salt

¼ pound fresh tuna

Juice of 1 lemon

The name of this seafood cocktail literally means "return to life," and for many people who party too hearty, it's a popular hangover cure. All along Mexican beaches, you see guys with machetes who crack the coconuts and then mix the seafood straight from the ocean right in front of you. While a freshly cracked coconut is ideal, you can substitute a can of unsweetened coconut milk for the meat and coconut liquid.

1. Rinse the shrimp shells well. In a small saucepan, heat the olive oil over medium-high heat, add the garlic, and sauté until soft, about 30 seconds. Add the shells; when they turn pink, add enough water to cover, and bring to a boil. Adjust the heat to low and simmer for 15 to 20 minutes. Drain the broth into a medium-size saucepan.

2. Bring the shrimp stock to a boil, add the shrimp, and poach until pink and just cooked through, about 1 minute. Strain the shrimp, cool completely, and slice in half lengthwise; refrigerate until ready to use.

3. Pour half of the lime juice into a small bowl. Blot the scallops, slice in half horizontally, and then into quarters vertically. Add them to the lime juice and refrigerate for 15 minutes.

4. Put the red onion in a small bowl of ice water and let it stand while you prepare the coconut base.

5. Carefully crack the coconut open using a large nail and hammer. Pour the coconut water into the jar of an electric blender. Scrape out the coconut meat with a spoon, add it to the jar, and blend until smooth and thick. Add the cilantro, reserving a few sprigs for the garnish, blend just until it turns pale green, and strain into a bowl.

6. Add the remaining lime juice to the coconut mixture. Drain the onion and add it along with the jalapeño, mint, and remaining cilantro, finely chopped, to the coconut base. Cut the avocado into small dice and add it, as well. Taste to adjust the seasonings, as necessary, with salt.

7. Drain the scallops and add them along with the shrimp to the base.

8. Cut the tuna into small dice and marinate it in the lemon juice for about 5 minutes before serving. Drain the tuna and carefully stir it into the coconut mixture. Return the mixture to the coconut base and serve in the coconut, over ice, or in small chilled martini glasses.

BAJA-STYLE FISH TACOS

TACOS DE PESCADO EN ESTILO DE BAJA

Yield: Serves 6

Mayonnaise Sauce (recipe below, right)
Vegetable oil, for frying
1 cup all-purpose flour
½ cup cornstarch
1 teaspoon garlic powder
1 ½ teaspoons teaspoon salt, divided
1 cup ice cold Mexican beer, such as Tecate
1 ½ pounds boneless cod, cut into 2-inch
   pieces
6 (4-inch) corn tortillas, warmed
2 cups shredded white cabbage
2 limes

Fish tacos are another Baja treat sold in stands at fish markets, where nice, large pieces of cod are fried to order and put into steaming hot tortillas. Then you go over to the salsa bar to put on your mayonnaise, cabbage, and salsa; sit or lean at the counter and enjoy them with an icy bottle of Tecate beer while you watch the sunset.

1. Make the Mayonnaise Sauce (below).

2. Fill a deep fat fryer or deep pot halfway with oil and heat until it measures 375°F on an instant-read thermometer.

3. In a bowl, sift together the flour, cornstarch, garlic powder, and ½ teaspoon of salt; whisk in the beer.

4. Sprinkle the cod with the remaining salt, dip the pieces into the prepared batter, letting any extra batter fall back into the bowl, and deep-fry them in batches, if necessary, until golden brown and cooked through, about 4 minutes. Blot on paper towels. Divide the pieces among the warm tortillas, drizzle with the mayonnaise sauce, top with a little shredded cabbage and a squeeze of lime to taste, and serve.

MAYONNAISE SAUCE

Yield: 1 ½ cups

1 cup mayonnaise
¼ cup milk
4 tablespoons freshly squeezed lemon juice
1 teaspoon garlic salt

Mix all ingredients.

SEA URCHIN TOSTADAS WITH DEVILED CUCUMBERS

TOSTADAS DE ERIZO A LA GUERRERENSE CON PEPINO EN DIABLADA

Yield: Serves 6

The roe of briny fresh sea urchins, one of my favorite foods, accompanied by Pepino en Diablada, as served at La Guerrerense, is among the most typical dishes of Baja. This is my taste memory of that version. You'll need about half of the Pepino en Diablada recipe. The remainder will keep in your refrigerator for a week.

1 cup *Pepino en Diablada* (recipe follows)

½ white onion, minced

1 tablespoon dry sherry

1 tablespoon freshly squeezed lemon juice

1 tablespoon chopped cilantro leaves

2 tablespoons extra-virgin olive oil

24 pieces sea urchin roe, available at specialty food seafood department or from sushi chefs to order

Salt and pepper

6 (4-inch) corn tortillas

Vegetable oil, to fry the tortillas

1. Prepare the *Pepino en Diablada.*

2. In a bowl, combine the onion, sherry, lemon juice, cilantro, and olive oil. Add the urchin roe, season with salt and pepper, and let marinate while you fry the tortillas in a small skillet in a little oil until golden and crisp. Top the warm tortillas with the urchin and serve with the *Pepino en Diablada* on the side.

DEVILED CUCUMBERS/PEPINO EN DIABLADA

Yield: 2 cups

1 hothouse cucumber

1 small shallot, finely diced

½ tablespoon minced *habanero* chile, seeded if desired

½ cup fresh mint leaves, chopped fairly fine

4 teaspoons rice vinegar

½ teaspoon salt

2 tablespoons olive oil

1. Peel the cucumber in strips for a striped effect; cut in half lengthwise, scoop out the seeds with a spoon, and cut crosswise into ¼-inch thick slices. Combine the cucumbers, shallots, *habanero*, and mint in a bowl.

2. In a small bowl, combine the vinegar and salt. Gradually whisk in the olive oil. Pour over the cucumbers, toss gently to combine, marinate for 15 minutes, and serve.

SHRIMP MEATBALLS

ALBONDIGAS DE CAMARON

Yield: Serves 4 (about 16 meatballs)

In Acapulco, fish meatballs are commonly served in a cone or basket with Cholula hot sauce (see sidebar below), a favorite condiment on virtually every table throughout Mexico. However, you can find plenty of great hot sauces today in supermarkets and specialty food stores, as well as in Latino grocery stores.

1 pound skinless red snapper fillets

2 large egg whites, beaten

1 teaspoon of salt

½ cup heavy cream

1 pound peeled and deveined shrimp, finely diced

¼ teaspoon ground nutmeg

Salt and freshly ground black pepper

Dash of Tabasco

Fish stock or water, for simmering

Hot sauce

1. Chill the work bowl and blade of a food processor until very cold. Combine the snapper, egg whites, and 1 teaspoon of salt in the bowl and purée until smooth. Slowly pour in the cream, adding more if necessary until the mixture is firm enough to form into balls. Stir the shrimp, nutmeg, additional salt, pepper, and Tabasco to taste into the meatball mixture.

2. Bring a pot of fish stock or water to a simmer. Test the consistency of the meatballs by adding a rounded tablespoon of the mixture to the water or fish stock, adding more egg white if the meatball doesn't hold together.

3. Drop rounded tablespoonfuls into the simmering stock and poach until cooked through, 5 to 6 minutes, turning once. Remove with a slotted spoon to a platter. Serve very hot with hot sauce.

 CHOLULA HOT SAUCE

CHOLULA IS A 2,500-YEAR-OLD CITY IN MEXICO THAT IS THE OLDEST INHABITED CITY IN CENTRAL AMERICA. THE HOT SAUCE WITH THE SAME NAME IS PRODUCED IN CHAPALA, AN HOUR FROM THE CITY OF GUADALAJARA. IT HAS A LIVELY BLEND OF RED PEPPERS, PIQUIN PEPPERS, AND SPICES THAT IS MEANT TO ENHANCE YOUR DINING EXPERIENCE RATHER THAN NUMB YOUR TASTE BUDS.

CLAMS WITH CHORIZO

ALMEJAS CON CHORIZO

Yield: Serves 1

2 teaspoons vegetable oil

2 to 4 large cloves garlic, thinly sliced

2 toasted *chiles de arbol*

3 ounces Mexico chorizo, casing removed and crumbled

10 littleneck clams, scrubbed

½ cup bottled clam juice

Salt

2 tablespoons unsalted butter

Freshly ground black pepper

1 teaspoon thinly sliced *epazote*

Combine clams with chorizo and abundant garlic and you get this intensely flavorful, one-dish meal that's not only remarkably satisfying but very easy to make. Be sure to serve crusty bread to sop up the delicious broth. While Spanish and Portuguese chorizo sausages are cured, Mexican chorizo is fresh and must always be cooked.

1. Heat the oil in a sauté pan over medium heat. Stir in the garlic and chiles and sauté until the garlic is transparent and lightly colored, about 2 minutes. Add the chorizo and sauté until cooked through, separating the pieces with a wooden spatula.

2. Add the clams, pour in the clam juice, and add a pinch of salt. Cover the pan and cook over high heat until the all the clams have opened, about 2 minutes. Remove the lid, swirl in the butter, and cook until the sauce is slightly reduced, about 3 minutes. Season to taste with salt and pepper, sprinkle in the *epazote*, and serve in a large, flat bowl with the broth. Discard any clams that do not open.

CRAB MASA TURNOVERS

MOLOTES DE JAIBA

Yield: Serves 6 (20 pieces)

FILLING

1 pound lump crabmeat, picked over

¼ cup homemade or high-quality purchased mayonnaise

¼ cup *crème fraîche* or sour cream

2 tablespoons chopped flat-leaf parsley

2 tablespoons snipped fresh chives

1 tablespoon Dijon mustard

2 teaspoons freshly squeezed lemon juice

2 teaspoon hot smoked paprika, such as *Pimentón de la Vera*

Salt and freshly ground black pepper

MOLOTES

1 pound *masa harina*

1 ¾ to 2 cups warm water

½ tablespoon salt

2 to 3 cups vegetable oil, for deep-fat frying

Coarse sea salt, to garnish

For a crispy treat, try these quickly fried, bullet-shaped turnovers filled with a smoky crabmeat mixture. Serve them with any salsa of your choice. For an even tastier version, purée Salsa Verde with an avocado for Tomatillo-Avocado Salsa (at right).

1. In a bowl, gently stir the crab, mayonnaise, *crème fraîche*, parsley, chives, mustard, lemon juice, and paprika together until just blended. Don't overmix. Season to taste with salt and pepper; set aside.

2. In a large bowl, mix the *masa harina*, 1 ¾ cups of water, and salt together into a smooth, uniform-textured dough that doesn't stick to your hands, about 10 minutes; slowly add more water if needed. Roll the dough into golf ball–size balls (about 2 ounces each).

3. Using a tortilla maker lined on the top and inside bottom with plastic wrap press each ball into a disk about 4 ½ to 5 inches in diameter. Otherwise, pat them out with your fingers. Fill each with a rounded tablespoon of the filling and seal the edges tightly, and form into a bullet shape.

4. Pour about 3 inches of oil into a large deep skillet or deep fat fryer and heat until hot, about 375°F on an instant-read thermometer. Add about 4 *molotes* at a time so the oil remains hot; cook until golden brown and hot in the center, about 3 minutes. Carefully remove with a slotted spoon, drain on paper towels, sprinkle with coarse salt, and serve. The *molotes* may be kept in a slow oven for up to 10 minutes.

TOMATILLO-AVOCADO SALSA

Yield: 3 cups

Prepare this salsa fresh each time before serving.

2 cups *Salsa Verde* (page 135)

1 ripe avocado, preferably Hass variety, peeled and pitted

Kosher salt

Make the *Salsa Verde*. In the jar of an electric blender, combine it with avocado and purée until smooth; season to taste with salt.

SHRIMP AND HOMINY STEW
POSOLE DE CAMARONES

Yield: Serves 4

This rich soup made with hominy and shrimp originated in the Mexican state of Jalisco and is customarily served on Christmas Eve after midnight mass. In Mexico, children parade around their neighborhoods dressed as pilgrims looking for a place to shelter the Holy Family. They are refused until finally they arrive at a neighbor's house—where traditional treats await them—or their parish church where mass is celebrated on Noche Buena.

1 cup Herbed *Salsa Verde* (recipe follows)

Lime Sea Salt, for garnish (recipe follows)

2 tablespoons olive oil, divided

1 cup chopped white onion

3 cloves garlic, minced

3 cups fish stock

2 tablespoons finely chopped sun-dried tomatoes in oil

1 tablespoon finely grated lime zest

1 pound uncooked medium shrimp, peeled and deveined

1 (15-ounce) can white hominy, rinsed and drained

Chopped cilantro, for garnish

Chopped white onion, for garnish

Chopped *jalapeños*, for garnish

Dried oregano, preferably Mexican, for garnish

1. Make the Herbed *Salsa Verde* (at right) and Lime Sea Salt (at right).

2. Heat 1 tablespoon of the oil in large saucepan over medium-high heat. Add the onion and sauté until tender, about 5 minutes. Add the garlic and stir for 30 seconds. Stir in the fish stock, Herbed *Salsa Verde*, sun-dried tomatoes, and lime zest and simmer for 5 minutes. Set aside.

3. Heat a large skillet over medium-high heat. Add the remaining oil and the shrimp and cook until lightly browned on both sides, about 3 minutes, turning once. Add the stock-salsa mixture and hominy and simmer until the seafood is just opaque in the center, about 3 minutes; season to taste with salt and pepper.

4. Serve in large, flat bowls with small bowls of cilantro, white onion, *jalapeños*, dried oregano, and Lime Sea Salt on the side.

HERBED *SALSA VERDE*

1 cup baby arugula leaves

¼ bunch flat-leaf parsley, coarsely chopped

Leaves from 2 sprigs marjoram, coarsely chopped

Leaves from 2 sprigs basil, coarsely chopped

Zest of 1 orange

1 anchovy fillet, rinsed well

1 clove garlic

½ teaspoon pepper

¼ teaspoon salt

¼ cup extra-virgin olive oil

Pulse the arugula leaves, parsley, marjoram, basil, orange zest, anchovy, garlic, pepper, salt, and olive oil in a food processor until blended and chunky-smooth.

LIME SEA SALT

Yield: 1 cup

Grated zest of 8 limes

4 tablespoons crushed dried *chile de árbol*

4 tablespoons coarse sea salt

2 tablespoons coriander seeds

Mash the ingredients together in a *molcajete* until combined.

RED POSOLE WITH OYSTERS
POSOLE ROJO CON OSTIONES

Yield: Serves 3 to 4

This red stew is from the Huasteca region that includes the northern part of Veracruz, as well as parts of the states of Puebla, Tamaulipas, San Luis Potosí, and Hidalgo. Because this area has been less influenced by Spanish conquerors or contemporary cuisine, they still use a lot of corn. Thus posole, or hominy, is popular. They also eat a lot of seafood, often with plenty of chiles. The sauce's intense red color and flavor are great complements to the oysters.

1 tablespoon unsalted butter

6 cloves garlic, thinly sliced, plus 2 additional cloves garlic

5 cups water, plus ½ cup boiling water

2 cups chicken stock

1 cup bottled clam juice

½ teaspoon dried oregano, preferably Mexican, crumbled

1 ounce dried *guajillo* chiles, stemmed and seeded

¼ large white onion, coarsely chopped

1 teaspoon salt

1 (15-ounce) can white hominy, rinsed and drained

1 quart shucked oysters, with their liquid

½ cup panko breadcrumbs

¾ cup vegetable oil

Accompaniments: Diced avocado, thinly sliced romaine lettuce, chopped white onion, sliced radishes, lime wedges, dried oregano, and dried hot red pepper flakes.

1. In a large, heavy soup pot, heat the butter over medium heat. Add the sliced garlic and sauté until translucent, about 4 minutes, stirring frequently. Pour in the 5 cups of water, the chicken stock, and clam juice and bring just to a boil. Skim the surface, add oregano, lower the heat, and simmer for 10 minutes.

2. Toast the chiles lightly, put them in a bowl with the ½ cup of boiling water, and soak for 30 minutes or until soft, turning occasionally. Transfer the chiles and their soaking liquid to the jar of an electric blender along with the onion, the 2 remaining garlic cloves, and salt; purée until smooth. Add the purée to the broth along with the hominy; season to taste with salt and simmer for 30 minutes. Posole may be made 2 days ahead to this point and covered and refrigerated.

3. Reheat the posole to a simmer, if necessary; add all but 8 oysters to the pot and simmer for 2 minutes more.

4. While the posole is simmering, dredge the remaining oysters in panko. In a 10-inch skillet, heat ½ inch of oil over high heat until hot but not smoking; fry the oysters in 3 or 4 batches until golden, 1 to 2 minutes per side. Using a slotted spoon, transfer the oysters to paper towels to drain. Serve the posole with fried oysters as a garnish along with bowls of the accompaniments.

SEAFOOD CASSEROLE
SERAPE DEL MAR

Yield: Serves 4

½ cup *Habanero* Salsa I (page 22)

½ pound octopus, cleaned

1 pound tomatoes, coarsely chopped

2 white onions, coarsely chopped

2 *poblano* chiles, seeds and membranes removed, coarsely chopped

½ cup firmly packed, coarsely chopped flat-leaf parsley

6 cloves garlic, divided

¼ cup, plus ½ cup olive oil

1 pound cleaned squid, cut into ½-inch pieces with tentacles reserved, soaked in buttermilk

8 jumbo shrimp, peeled and sliced in half lengthwise

Sea salt

2 large bay leaves

1 tablespoon squid ink diluted in ¼ cup rice vinegar

1 teaspoon sugar

Freshly ground black pepper

All-purpose flour, for dredging

8 (6-inch) corn tortillas

Crema

Chopped flat-leaf parsley

The city of Veracruz, on the Gulf of Mexico, is a major fishing port with some of the best and freshest seafood imaginable. This seafood stew reminds me of a serape, the colorful woven Mexican blanket or shawl that has black threads as the underlying color with vibrant accent colors. It is made with squid ink and seafood, and is spooned over tortillas.

1. Prepare the *Habanero* Salsa I and keep warm.

2. Bring a pot of water to a boil. Add the octopus, lower the heat to a gentle simmer, and cook until the octopus is tender, about 1 hour, adding water as needed to keep octopus covered. Remove and cut into ½-inch pieces; cover and set aside.

3. In the jar of an electric blender, combine the tomatoes, onion, chiles, parsley, and 2 of the garlic cloves; blend for a few seconds to make a chunky-smooth purée. Set aside.

4. Thinly slice the remaining garlic. Heat the ¼ cup of oil in a medium-size skillet over medium heat; add one fourth of the sliced garlic and fry until golden brown. Remove the garlic with a slotted spoon and discard.

5. Drain the squid. Add the remaining sliced garlic to the oil in the skillet along with the squid, octopus, and shrimp; sprinkle with salt and quickly sauté for 2 to 3 minutes, tossing from time to time. Add the tomato purée, bay leaves, squid ink, sugar, and pepper to taste; cook over high heat for about 6 minutes to reduce the sauce. The seafood should be tender. Keep warm.

6. Heat the remaining ½ cup of oil in a large skillet. Dredge the tentacles in flour. Working in pairs, cook the tentacles until crispy and golden, about 2 minutes; drain on paper towels.

7. Put 1 tortilla in the bottom of each of 4 flat bowls and ladle ¼ cup of the sauce over and around each tortilla. Top each tortilla with ¾ cup of the seafood mixture. Add another tortilla and spoon ¼ cup of sauce on top. Drizzle with *crema*, add the fried tentacles in the center of the serape, and sprinkle with parsley.

TUMBLED RICE
ARROZ A LA TUMBADA

Yield: Serves 8

The word tumbada means "tumbled" and everything in this dish is just that: the seafood and rice are basically thrown together. It's a colorful, casual dish similar to Spanish paella.

6 tablespoons olive oil

8 cloves garlic, thinly sliced

2 red bell peppers, seeds and membranes removed, cut in ¼-inch dice

1 white onion, cut into ¼-inch dice

2 tablespoons hot smoked paprika, such as *pimentón de la Vera*

3 tablespoons squid ink, available online or at some Italian grocers

3 cups short grain rice, such as *bomba* or Arborio

8 cups fish stock or clam juice, heated

2 cups diced fresh or canned tomatoes

1 cup sliced scallions, including green parts

1 cup dry white wine

1 ½ pounds fresh squid, cleaned and cut into ¼-inch rings

1 pound jumbo shrimp, peeled and deveined

1 pound Prince Edward Island or other farmed mussels, scrubbed

½ pound manila clams, scrubbed and debearded

½ pound uncooked lobster meat, sliced (see "Note")

1 cup mayonnaise

¼ cup cracked black pepper

Salt and freshly ground black pepper

1. In a very large, deep casserole, heat the oil over medium-high heat until hot and shimmering. Add the garlic, peppers, onion, and paprika; cook until the vegetables are soft and translucent, about 4 minutes, stirring occasionally. Add the squid ink and rice and continue to cook until the rice is translucent, about 5 minutes.

2. Pour in the fish stock and bring to a boil; lower the heat, cover the pan, and cook until the rice is al dente and liquid has been absorbed, about 20 minutes. The recipe can be made ahead to this point and then reheated later with a little extra stock.

3. While the rice is cooking, in a large skillet, bring the tomatoes, scallions, and white wine to a simmer. Add the squid, shrimp, mussels, clams, and lobster meat to the pan and gently cook until just done, 8 to 10 minutes, stirring frequently.

4. In a bowl, blend the mayonnaise with the black pepper.

5. Turn the rice into an attractive serving dish, bowl, or casserole; add the fish and stir to mix. Season to taste with salt and pepper and serve with a little mayonnaise drizzled on top. Pass the extra mayonnaise at the table.

NOTE: LOBSTER MEAT CAN BE EASILY REMOVED FROM THE SHELL BY BLANCHING THE LOBSTER IN BOILING WATER FOR 30 SECONDS AND THEN SHOCKING IT IN ICE WATER. THE MEAT PULLS AWAY FROM THE SHELL BUT REMAINS ESSENTIALLY RAW.

CHAPTER SEVEN

POULTRY/AVES

CHICKEN VEGETABLE SOUP
CALDO TLALPENO

Yield: Serves 8

Even if you think your abuela's (grandmother's) chicken soup is the best, you must try this version. At Dos Caminos, it draws great raves! And grandma knows best: it's great for a cold or anything else that ails you, as well as being a bowl of satisfying comfort food. You can always add leftover chicken to this colorful elixir.

8 cups chicken stock

1 whole chicken breast, about 1 ¼ pounds with skin and bones

1 ½ tablespoons vegetable or olive oil

1 large white onion, halved lengthwise and thinly sliced lengthwise

2 carrots, peeled and cut into ⅛-inch-thick slices

1 zucchini, cut into ¼-inch-thick slices

2 cups cooked chickpeas or rinsed and drained canned chickpeas

2 whole canned *chipotles en adobo*, seeded and cut into strips

Salt and freshly ground black pepper

1 avocado, preferably Hass variety, for garnish

8 lime wedges, for garnish

1. In a large saucepan, bring the stock just to a boil. Add the chicken and gently simmer until the chicken is just cooked through, about 15 minutes; remove from the heat and let the chicken cool in the broth.

2. Transfer the chicken to a cutting board, reserving the broth; discard the skin and bones. Shred the chicken, cover it, and refrigerate.

3. In a large, heavy saucepan, heat the oil over medium-high heat. Add the onion and cook until softened, stirring occasionally. Add the carrots and zucchini, cook for 1 minute, stir in the reserved broth and chickpeas, and simmer until the carrots are just tender, about 8 minutes. The soup and the chicken may be prepared up to this point a day in advance and kept covered and refrigerated.

4. Stir the reserved chicken into the soup along with the chiles and salt and pepper to taste; simmer gently until the chicken is heated through.

5. Peel and slice the avocado. Ladle the soup into wide soup bowls and garnish with avocado slices and a lime wedge.

CHICKEN BAKED IN PAPER

MIXIOTE DE POLLO

Yield: Serves 6

6 *ancho* chiles, stemmed and seeded

8 *guajillo* chiles, stemmed and seeded

4 *pasilla* chiles, stemmed and seeded

8 whole cloves

1 bay leaf

½ teaspoon dried oregano, preferably Mexican

⅛ teaspoon cumin seeds

⅛ teaspoon dried marjoram

⅛ teaspoon dried thyme

4 cloves garlic

1 tablespoon white vinegar

2 teaspoons kosher salt

6 chicken drumstick-thigh quarters, cut at the joint

6 *mixiotes* or enough parchment paper for 3 (16 inch) squares

6 fresh or dried avocado leaves

Warm corn tortillas or cooked white rice, for serving

Mixiotes are the outermost layers of young maguey plant leaves called pencas. The membranes are removed in sheets and used to wrap little bundles of marinated meats and chiles that are then steamed, as you would tamales. This recipe was taught to me in Puebla by the mother of my former sous chef Alejandro Sanchez. If you can't find mixiotes, you can use banana leaves, parchment paper, or even plastic sandwich bags wrapped in aluminum foil.

1. In a small pot, rehydrate the *ancho*, *guajillo*, and *pasilla* chiles in just enough hot water to cover; soak until tender and drain, reserving the soaking liquid.

2. In the jar of an electric blender, finely grind the cloves, bay leaf, oregano, cumin seeds, marjoram, and thyme; add the drained chiles, garlic, vinegar, salt, and ½ cup of the chile soaking liquid and purée until smooth.

3. Scrape the mixture into a large bowl or glass baking dish, add the chicken, and marinate in the refrigerator for at least 2 hours, but preferably overnight.

4. If using the *mixiotes*, soak them for 5 to 10 minutes until pliable; otherwise cut 3 16 x 16-inch parchment paper squares.

5. Put a drumstick, thigh, and an avocado leaf in the center of each *mixiote* or square. Bring the four corners together, and tie with string using a slipknot.

6. Fill a large, deep pan with enough water to come up to the bottom of a steamer insert and bring to a simmer. A simple bamboo steamer works well, as will an inverted colander in a large stockpot. Put the packets in the insert and steam for 1 hour. To serve, remove the string and open the parchment paper or *mixiote*, folding it under slightly. Serve with warm corn tortillas on the side.

CHICKEN TINGA POBLANO

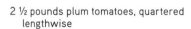

TINGA DE POLLO POBLANA

Yield: Serves 3 to 4

2 ½ pounds plum tomatoes, quartered lengthwise

Vegetable oil

1 white onion, sliced, plus ½ small onion, chopped

1 cup chicken stock

½ (6-ounce) cone *piloncillo*

2 canned *chipotles en adobo*

¼ cup rice vinegar

2 ½ tablespoons chopped fresh thyme leaves

2 bay leaves, divided

1 (3 ½-pound) chicken, cut into pieces

1 clove garlic

1 small carrot, chopped

1 small stalk celery, chopped

½ tablespoon fresh oregano leaves

1 teaspoon cracked black peppercorns

Corn tortillas, warmed

We all need a homey, satisfying chicken stew in our reper-toire. This one—I consider it like Mexican sweet and sour chicken—more than fits that bill with tender shredded chicken in a mildly spicy tomato-chipotle sauce. When I say "shred," I prefer fairly coarse strips here. You can also serve this over rice or with sopes (page 161).

1. Preheat the oven to 300˚F.

2. Toss the tomatoes with a little oil and roast in a flat pan until soft and golden, about 1 hour. Meanwhile, heat 1 teaspoon of oil in a small skillet, add the sliced onion, and cook until golden brown, stirring occasionally; combine the onion in a nonreactive pan with the chicken stock, *piloncillo*, canned *chipotles*, vinegar, thyme, and 1 bay leaf; cook over low heat for 20 minutes to blend the flavors.

3. While the tomatoes are roasting, in a large casserole, com-bine the chicken with enough water to cover along with the chopped onion, garlic, remaining bay leaf, carrot, celery, oreg-ano, and pepper; bring to a boil, lower the heat, and simmer until the meat is tender, about 45 minutes. Remove the chicken from the liquid, let it cool slightly, take the meat off the bones, and coarsely shred with two forks. Set aside.

4. When the tomatoes are done, stir them into the sauce; add the shredded chicken, simmer to blend the flavors, and season to taste with salt and pepper. Serve with warm tortillas.

DROWNED CHICKEN SANDWICHES
TORTAS AHOGADAS

Yield: Serves 4

In this Mexican version of the Sloppy Joe, flavorful Chicken Tinga (page 144) is ahogada or "drowned" under smoky Roasted Tomato-Chipotle Salsa.

2 cups My Refried Beans (page 86)

1 cup Roasted Tomato-*Chipotle* Salsa (page 18)

1 pound *Tinga de Pollo Poblana* (recipe at left)

4 torta rolls, cut in half horizontally

2 tomatoes, sliced crosswise

2 avocados, preferably Hass variety, peeled and sliced

1 red onion, thinly sliced

Leaves of 2 sprigs fresh oregano

1. Prepare the My Refried Beans and Roasted Tomato-*Chipotle* Salsa and keep warm. Heat the Chicken Tinga.

2. Spread the refried beans on the bottom portion of each torta roll. Spoon the chicken over the refried beans. Top with tomato, avocado, and onion; sprinkle on the oregano, and add ¼ cup salsa to the top of each torta roll to each to "drown" the sandwiches.

 CHICKEN TINGA

I DISCOVERED IN PUEBLA AND HAVE FOUND THAT THE CHICKEN'S SPICY-SMOKY FLAVOR GETS BETTER THE LONGER IT SITS, SO I ALWAYS MAKE EXTRAS FOR SANDWICHES.

CHICKEN TACOS
CHICKEN AL CARBON TACOS
Serves 8

Chicken tacos are always a crowd pleaser and great for a lazy summer evening because they are so easy to make. Serve with some fresh salsa, refried beans, and Mexican rice for a weekend fiesta.

Marinade (recipe follows)
2 pounds chicken legs and thighs
32 small corn tortillas
Pico de Gallo (page 18)
Crema for garnish
Grated *Cotija* cheese for garnish
Cilantro leaves for garnish

1. Rub the marinade all over the chicken. Place in a glass baking dish, cover and refrigerate at least 1 hour or preferably overnight.

2. Heat the oven to 350°F. Transfer the chicken to a roasting pan. Roast for about 45 minutes, or until the meat pulls away easily from the bone. Set the chicken aside to cool and reserve the cooking juices.

3. When the chicken is cool, remove and discard the skin and bones and shred the meat into large pieces. Refrigerate the chicken if you do not plan to use it right away.

4. To serve use the cooking juices to reheat the chicken in a warm oven.

5. Toast each tortilla in a nonstick pan over medium heat for about 30 seconds on each side. Wrap in a towel to keep warm.

6. For each taco, divide the warm chicken and place on top of a tortilla. Top with *pico de gallo*, *crema*, *Cotija* cheese, and chopped cilantro.

MARINADE

⅔ cup freshly squeezed orange
 juice

⅓ cup freshly squeezed lime
 juice

¼ cup achiote paste

3 jalapeno peppers

8 garlic cloves, peeled

2 tablespoons Maggi sauce

1 tablespoon whole black peppercorns

1 tablespoon salt

1 bunch cilantro

Combine all the ingredients
in a blender and puree until
smooth.

ROASTED CHICKEN FLAUTAS

FLAUTAS DE POLLO

These tasty flautas or "flutes" are made with juicy baked and shredded chicken wrapped in corn tortillas and fried. They are sometimes called taquitos.

Yield: Serves 4 to 6 as an entrée;
6 to 8 as an *antojito* (appetizer)

1 cup Meat Spice Rub (recipe follows)
1 cup apple juice
2 ½ pounds boneless skinless chicken thighs
Salt
12 (6-inch) corn tortillas
Vegetable oil
Pico de Gallo (page 18)
Crumbled *queso fresco*
Crema

1. Make the Meat Spice Rub (at right) and combine it with the apple juice, stirring to blend. Scrape the mixture into a resealable plastic bag, add the chicken, turning to cover, and marinate overnight.

2. Preheat the oven to 350˚F.

3. Space the thighs evenly on a rack on a sheet pan and bake until cooked through, about 45 minutes. Remove from the oven, cool, and shred the chicken by hand before it has completely cooled; season to taste with salt. Lightly brush the tortillas with oil, spoon ¼ cup of filling in each, roll up, and secure with a pair of toothpicks.

4. Prepare the *Pico de Gallo*.

5. Use a deep fryer or a large skillet filled with enough oil to measure 1 inch deep and heat to 375˚F on an instant-read thermometer. Drop 2 or 3 flautas at a time into the hot oil and cook until crispy. If using a skillet, turn the flautas so they become crisp and golden on all sides, 3 to 5 minutes. Drain on paper towels, remove the toothpicks, and serve on a small oval taco plate, folded side down. Sprinkle with crumbled *queso fresco*, *Pico de Gallo*, and a drizzle of *crema*.

MEAT SPICE RUB

Yield: about 1 ¼ cups

½ cup firmly packed dark brown
    sugar

¼ cup turbinado sugar

¼ cup salt

2 tablespoons paprika

½ tablespoon freshly ground
    black pepper

½ tablespoon white pepper

½ tablespoon onion powder

½ tablespoon garlic powder

½ teaspoon ground cumin

½ teaspoon ground celery seed

½ teaspoon *ancho* chile powder

¼ teaspoon *chile de arbol* powder

Combine all of the spice rub
ingredients in a bowl and mix
well.

SHREDDED YUCATÁN-STYLE CHICKEN

POLLO EN ESCABECHE ORIENTAL

Yield: Serves 3 to 4

Dishes in escabeche refer to foods marinated and/or cooked in vinegar. It was an early technique of cooking foods to preserve them before the days of refrigeration. These dishes are common in the Yucatán where, because of its proximity to the Gulf, they were probably introduced by the early Spanish settlers.

Spice Paste (recipe follows)

Lime-Cured Onions (recipe follows)

7 cups water

3 pounds boneless skinless chicken thighs

2 bay leaves

1 teaspoon salt

½ teaspoon whole cumin seeds

½ teaspoon dried oregano, preferably Mexican

¼ teaspoon cracked black peppercorns

6 cloves garlic, minced

Flour, for dusting

2 cups lard, for frying

4 *chiles gueros*, or spicy pepperoncini, cut into thin strips

1 tablespoon cider vinegar

1. Make the Spice Paste and the Lime-Cured Onions (at right).

2. In a large pot, bring water to a boil, add the chicken, and simmer for a few minutes, skimming the surface. Add the bay leaves, salt, cumin, oregano, peppercorns, and garlic; partially cover the pot with foil or a lid and simmer until the chicken is tender, about 20 minutes. Cool the chicken in the broth; remove and transfer the pieces, flesh side up, to a clean surface. Reserve the broth.

3. When the chicken has dried, rub 1 tablespoon of Spice Paste on the flesh side of each thigh and let stand for 1 hour.

4. Lightly dust the spice-covered side of the chicken with flour. Heat the lard in a large skillet over medium-high heat until hot but not smoking. Add the thighs, spice-covered side down; add 1 cup of the Lime-Cured Onions and the *chiles gueros*. Cook about 5 minutes until the onions have softened.

5. Add the vinegar, 3 cups of the reserved cooking broth, and ½ tablespoon of the seasoning paste. Simmer a few minutes to combine the flavors. Remove the thighs and, when cool enough to handle, shred not too finely and then return the chicken to the pan and stir to blend. Adjust the salt, if necessary.

SPICE PASTE

3 allspice berries

3 whole cloves

2 teaspoons dried oregano, preferably Mexican

1 teaspoon black peppercorns

¼ teaspoon whole cumin seeds

½ teaspoon salt

12 cloves roasted garlic

1 tablespoon cider vinegar

1 teaspoon flour, plus flour for dusting chicken

Grind the allspice, cloves, oregano, peppercorns, and cumin in a spice grinder and transfer to a *molcajete* with the salt. Add the garlic and mash into a smooth paste. Work in the vinegar and flour and let stand for at least 2 hours before using.

LIME-CURED ONIONS

1 white onion, very thinly sliced

Juice of 3 limes

½ bunch cilantro, leaves and a few stems, finely julienned

1 teaspoon dried oregano, preferably Mexican

I teaspoon salt

In a bowl, combine the onion, lime juice, cilantro, oregano, and salt; marinate for at least 2 hours.

COOKING TIP

IF YOU HAVE LEFTOVERS, SAVE ABOUT 2 CUPS FOR PANUCHOS YUCATECOS (PAGE 152). I THINK THE LIME-CURED ONIONS ARE A FLAVORFUL CONDIMENT FOR TACOS AND GRILLED MEATS, AS WELL.

TORTILLAS STUFFED WITH SHREDDED YUCATÁN-STYLE CHICKEN AND PICKLED RED ONIONS

PANUCHOS YUCATECOS CON POLLO EN ESCABECHE

Yield: Makes 12 pieces

2 cups leftover *Pollo En Escabeche Oriental* (page 150), warmed

1 cup Roasted Tomato-*Chipotle* Salsa (page 86), warmed

¼ cup My Refried Beans (page 86) or rinsed and drained canned black beans, puréed

1 cup Pickled Red Onions (recipe follows)

2 cups *masa harina*

1 ¼ cups warm water

½ teaspoon salt

Vegetable oil or lard

1 avocado, preferably Hass variety, peeled, seeded, and sliced

Panuchos are among the most traditional and popular appetizers in the Yucatán Peninsula. When these tortillas are fried, they puff up so they can be split and filled. Here the bean mixture is spooned inside with the tasty shredded chicken served on top.

1. Prepare the *Pollo en Escabeche Oriental*, Roasted Tomato-*Chipotle* Salsa, My Refried Beans, as needed, and the Pickled Red Onions.

2. In a large bowl, stir the *masa harina*, water, and salt together until smooth. The dough should be slightly sticky and form a ball when pressed together. To test, flatten a small piece of dough between your palms. If the edges crack, add water, a tablespoon at a time, until a test piece does not crack.

3. Divide the *masa* into 12 pieces and form each into a ball. Press each into a 4-inch circle. Heat a griddle or lightly oiled large skillet; cook the tortillas over medium-high heat, turning once, until they are puffed and lightly colored, and remove. When they are cool enough to handle, pick up each puffed tortilla and make a 1 ½-inch-long slit about ¼ inch from the edge to make a pocket, being careful not to cut all the way through the tortilla.

4. Stuff 2 teaspoons of My Refried Beans or bean purée in each pocket. Flatten to seal and spread the beans evenly. Reserve the tortillas on a tray covered with a barely dampened cloth.

5. In a large skillet, add enough vegetable oil or lard to measure 1 inch deep and heat over medium-high heat to 375°F on an instant-read thermometer. Add three stuffed tortillas at a time and cook until they are slightly crisp around the edges but still pliable, turning once, about 2 to 3 minutes; drain on

paper towels. Top each tortilla with a scant tablespoon of Roasted Tomato-*Chipotle* Salsa. Spoon about 2 tablespoons chicken and 1 teaspoon Pickled Red Onions on each, and top with a small avocado slice.

PICKLED RED ONIONS

1 red onion, thinly sliced
Salt
2 cloves garlic, chopped
½ teaspoon dried oregano
¼ teaspoon freshly ground black pepper
¼ teaspoon ground cumin seeds
⅓ cup cider vinegar

1. In a nonreactive saucepan, combine the onions, a pinch of salt, and water to cover; bring to a boil, cook for 1 minute, and drain. Meanwhile, grind the oregano, black pepper, and cumin in a spice grinder or *molcajete*.

2. In the same pan, combine the vinegar, garlic, oregano, pepper, cumin, and onions. Add enough water to cover the onions and bring to a boil; cook for 3 minutes and transfer to a bowl.

PANUCHOS ARE A GREAT
VEHICLE FOR EATING COOKED
MEATS LIKE CHICKEN TINGA,
SHREDDED SHORT RIBS, OR
LAMB. THIS RECIPE IS EASY TO
MAKE WITH LEFTOVERS.

CHICKEN PICADILLO TAMALES

TAMALES CON PICADILLO DE POLLO

Yield: Serves 4 (8 tamales)

These tamales will appeal to all of your senses. Not only are they colorful—the chicken is joined by carrots, beans, potato, and zucchini—but the tangy-sweet and spicy tomato sauce includes onions, almonds, raisins, vinegar, and jalapeños, so the texture is satisfying, as well. Serve as is, or with Salsa Verde, Mole Poblano, or any other salsa in the "Salsas y Condimentos" chapter.

½ pound dried cornhusks

1 cup *masa harina*

¾ cup warm water

½ cup plus 1 tablespoon lard, divided

½ cup chicken stock

2 tablespoons vegetable oil

1 cup diced carrots

1 cup diced green beans

1 cup diced potato

1 cup diced zucchini

1 medium tomato puréed with ½ large white onion

2 small whole chicken breasts, cooked and shredded

3 pickled *jalapeños*, seeds and membranes removed, minced

¼ cup blanched sliced almonds

¼ cup golden raisins

1 tablespoon red wine vinegar

1 tablespoon sugar

¼ teaspoon cinnamon

1. In a bowl, cover the cornhusks with warm water and soak to soften, at least 30 minutes.

2. For the tamales, moisten the *masa* with the warm water and set aside. Beat the ½ cup of lard in a stand mixer until creamy and fluffy, about 20 minutes. Fold in the *masa* mixture and the chicken stock, mix well, and set aside.

3. In a large skillet, heat the oil over medium-high heat until hot. Stir in the carrot, green beans, potato, and zucchini and sauté until al dente; remove and reserve.

4. Heat the remaining tablespoon of lard in a large pan over medium-high heat; add the tomato-onion purée and cook for 5 minutes. Stir in the reserved vegetables and chicken; add the *jalapeños*, almonds, raisins, vinegar, sugar, and cinnamon and simmer for 2 to 3 minutes to blend the flavors. Remove from the heat, and reserve.

5. To assemble the tamales, open the cornhusks and place 2 tablespoons of dough in the center of the cornhusk. Spread out into an oval shape, leaving about an inch from the edges. Spoon 2 tablespoons of the filling in the center. Fold the sides of the husk over and secure with a piece of string or piece of the husk (page 155). Repeat the process until all the tamales are rolled.

TAMALES (STEP BY STEP)

6. In a large double boiler with a steamer insert, bring the water to a boil. Add the tamales, in layers if necessary, leaving space for the steam to reach all of the tamales; steam for 40 to 45 minutes until done. Test by opening up one tamale; if it releases easily, the tamales are done. Do not overcook. Remove the tamales from the steamer and allow them to stand for 5 minutes. Then open them and serve.

TAMAL DE CAZUELA

Yield: Serves 4 to 6

This oversized tamale made in a round casserole can be prepared ahead and cut into wedges; its dramatic presentation is a great addition to a family gathering or potluck supper.

1 pound *masa harina* for tamales

5 cups water

1 ½ cups lard

2 tablespoons salt, divided

2 pounds boneless skinless chicken thighs

1 cup chicken stock

6 *guajillo* chiles

6 *ancho* chiles

4 cloves garlic

½ medium white onion, coarsely chopped

5 cloves

1 teaspoon dried oregano, preferably Mexican

½ teaspoon ground cumin

4 sprigs fresh *epazote*

Banana leaves

18 fresh or dried *hoja santa* leaves or banana leaves (see pages 272–273)

1. Combine the *masa harina* and water, stirring with your hands; knead the *masa* until thoroughly combined and let it rest in the refrigerator for 30 minutes. Remove, knead in the lard and 1 tablespoon salt, and continue to knead for 5 minutes more.

2. While the *masa* rests, simmer the chicken thighs in the chicken stock in a skillet until cooked through, about 30 minutes; remove the chicken and, when cool enough to handle, shred with two forks. Reserve the broth.

3. In a large saucepan, add enough water to just cover the *guajillo* and *ancho* chiles; bring to simmer for 5 minutes, turn off the heat, and let the chiles cool completely in the water. Transfer the chiles to the jar of an electric blender. Add the garlic, onion, cloves, oregano, cumin, and reserved chicken broth and blend until smooth. Strain into a saucepan, add the remaining 1 tablespoon salt and *epazote*, and simmer for 15 minutes. Whisk ½ cup of the *masa* into the sauce and continue to stir until the mixture thickens slightly.

4. Preheat the oven to 375˚F.

5. Cover the bottom of a deep 9-inch round casserole with banana leaves, shiny side up, ensuring that the entire bottom is covered and the leaves go all the way up the sides of the dish. Arrange 6 *hoja santa* leaves over the banana leaves inside the casserole.

TAMAL DE CAZUELA (STEP BY STEP)

6. Spread about a third of the *masa* over the *hoja santa* leaves, followed by half the chiles and the chicken. Repeat with more *hoja santa* leaves, *masa*, chiles, and chicken. Add a final layer of *masa* on top, taking care that it covers the edges of the casserole, then the last of the *hoja santa* leaves on top; cover with a piece of banana leaf. Fold the remaining banana leaves in over the top and seal the casserole with aluminum foil. Bake for about 1 hour until completely cooked. Remove from oven, open the banana leaves at table so people can see the interior, and cut into wedges.

Oaxaca Travel Diary

Our flight from New York through Mexico City to Oaxaca, with the connection, takes eight hours before we arrive at Hotel Camino Real Oaxaca. The spectacularly restored sixteenth-century convent is laid out around several courtyards with breathtaking bougainvillea and hibiscus gardens and unique fountains, including one formerly used by the nuns to wash their clothes. There is a special sense of serenity here, no doubt due to its former tenancy.

After freshening up, we head to the hotel's bar, Las Novicias, formerly the convent's library, where we are surrounded by ancient texts. It's our first opportunity to sample mezcal, the indigenous spirit of Oaxaca. Not to be confused with tequila—although it does come from the agave plant—mezcal is produced in a very different manner that results in a smoky, complex flavor unlike anything else.

I'm happy because I have a terrible cold and the Mexicans consider mezcal to be medicinal. A popular saying is *"para todo mal mescal—para todo bien tambien"* or "for everything bad, drink mezcal, and for everything good, drink mezcal." I'm not one to argue with this traditional practice, so we sip our mezcal and order a traditional Oaxacan botana or appetizer plate with a selection of local specialties like the famous quesillo, a cheese from the nearby valley of Etla that is very similar to fresh mozzarella.

It also has chorizo, a spicy pork sausage; tasajo, or air-dried beef; morcilla, blood sausage; and the quintessential Oaxacan snack, chapulines, dried grasshoppers toasted with chile and lime. They're pretty intimidating to look at but sublime when eaten in a taco with a little guacamole and hot salsa. Talk about great texture!

We move on to the zócalo, the town square, which is surrounded by a number of restaurants. Our choice is El Asador Vasco for its selection of Basque and Oaxacan dishes, and for the wonderful live music performed by local students dressed as traditional Spanish minstrels. We eat a variety of local specialties as well as some Basque dishes. The standout is the spectacular Tamal de Cazuela, a delicious tamale casserole.

CHOPPED CHICKEN LIVER
HIGADITOS

Yield: Serves 4 to 6

Some people think chicken livers are a bit of heaven; others don't care for them. I'm in that first group along with many Mexicans who really get excited about them. Try them as they're done here and I think you'll like them. This great hors d'oeuvre is not your deli's chopped liver, but the flat Matzo Sopes, or fried cakes, add a grandmotherly touch. Mexico City has one of the largest Jewish populations in the world. At Dos Caminos, we like to serve special foods to honor their holidays as they would be prepared in Mexico.

2 pounds chicken livers, cleaned

1 quart whole milk, for soaking

Matzo Sopes (recipe follows)

8 tablespoons (1 stick) unsalted butter

6 cloves garlic, minced

2 medium white onions, diced

4 anchovy fillets, rinsed, patted dry, and chopped

½ cup dry white wine, divided

½ cup chicken stock

Grated zest of 1 orange

¼ cup sherry vinegar

¼ cup honey

2 tablespoons chopped *chipotles en adobo*

6 hard-cooked eggs, finely chopped, 2 reserved for garnish

¼ cup mayonnaise

Salt and freshly ground black pepper

TO GARNISH

Minced red onion

Chopped cilantro

Chopped flat-leaf parsley

Hard boiled egg, chopped, yolk and white separate

Sliced pickled *jalapeños*

1. In a large bowl, soak the livers in milk for 30 minutes.

2. Prepare the *Matzo Sopes* (at right).

3. Melt the butter in a large skillet over medium heat. Stir in the garlic, onions, and anchovies and sauté until the onion is tender but not browned, mashing the anchovies with a fork, about 3 minutes.

4. Drain the livers. Increase the heat to medium-high, add the chicken livers, and sauté until golden brown, about 4 minutes. Add ¼ cup of the wine and cook until most of the liquid has evaporated. Stir in the chicken stock and simmer until the livers are cooked through and the liquid is reduced by half, breaking up the livers with a fork, about 10 minutes. Cool slightly.

5. Transfer the mix to the container of a food processor, and pulse until the livers are coarsely puréed. Add the orange zest, vinegar, honey, *chipotles*, 4 of the eggs, the mayonnaise, and the remaining ¼ cup wine; pulse just to blend and season to taste with salt and pepper. Serve the chopped liver atop *Matzo Sopes*. Sprinkle with a generous amount of red onion, cilantro, parsley, chopped eggs, and *jalapeños*.

MATZO SOPES

Yield: 16 sopes

1 cup matzo meal, ground to the
  consistency of flour
1 cup water
½ teaspoon salt
1 tablespoon vegetable oil, to grease the pan

1. In a bowl, combine the matzo meal,
water, and salt and mix by hand to the
consistency of *masa*.

2. Wet your hands and mold the *sopes*
into 16 small balls. Pat each ball into a
3-inch patty; place on waxed paper.

3. Heat a comal or large, heavy skillet
over medium-high heat until hot. Brush
with oil. Add the *sopes* and cook for
2 minutes on each side, turning once.
Remove and serve.

CHILES STUFFED WITH SPICY GROUND TURKEY

CHILES RELLENOS CON PICADILLO DE PAVO

Yield: 8 chiles rellenos

Roasted Tomato-*Chipotle* Salsa
   (page 18)

1 tablespoon vegetable oil

3 cloves garlic, minced

1 white onion, finely chopped

1 green bell pepper, seeds and membranes
   removed, finely chopped

¼ cup *ancho* chile powder

1 cup tomato paste

1 pound ground turkey

¼ cup dry sherry

2 cups tomato sauce

1 potato, peeled, cut into tiny cubes, and fried

½ cup diced dried apricots

½ cup sliced green olives

½ cup toasted sliced almonds

¼ cup golden raisins

1 teaspoon salt

½ teaspoon Tabasco sauce

8 *poblano* chiles, roasted, peeled, slit lengthwise, and seeded

All-purpose flour seasoned with salt and
   pepper, for dredging

5 large eggs, separated

Vegetable oil or lard, for frying

Turkeys are a New World bird, and one variety is known to have been domesticated by the Aztecs in the Yucatán forests. When I was looking for healthy alternatives with which to stuff chiles rellenos, I decided this Mexican native was an ideal choice.

1. Prepare the Roasted Tomato-*Chipotle* Salsa and keep warm.

2. In a large skillet, combine the oil, garlic, onion, and green pepper; cover and sweat over medium heat until soft, 6 to 7 minutes. Stir in the chile powder, tomato paste, and turkey sauté until cooked through, separating the pieces with a wooden spatula.

3. Pour in the sherry and tomato sauce, stirring up browned bits; remove from the heat stir in the potato, apricots, olives, almonds, raisins, salt, and Tabasco. Simmer briefly and taste to adjust.

4. Stuff each chile with about ½ cup of filling, press the opening together tightly, and dust with flour.

5. In a bowl, beat the egg whites until stiff; in a separate bowl, beat the yolks slightly with a pinch of salt and gently fold the yolks into the whites to make the batter.

6. Pour enough oil or melt enough lard in a large skillet to measure 1 inch deep; heat over medium-high heat until the fat registers 375°F on an instant-read thermometer.

7. Dip the chiles in the batter and fry until golden, 2 to 3 minutes on each side, turning to color both sides. While they are frying, carefully spoon some of the hot oil over the parts of the chiles along the sides that may not be directly touching the oil, so they get cooked evenly. Remove and drain on paper towels.

8. Spoon ½ cup of Roasted Tomato-*Chipotle* Salsa in the bottom of each of 4 shallow bowls or plates and lay chiles on top.

CHILES STUFFED WITH CHEESE
CHILES RELLENOS CON QUESO

Yield: 8 chiles rellenos

4 cups *queso Oaxaca*, pulled

½ cup *epazote*, thinly julienned

8 *poblano* chiles, roasted, peeled, slit lengthwise, and seeded

All-purpose flour seasoned with salt and pepper, for dredging

5 large eggs, separated

Vegetable oil or lard for frying

1. Combine the *queso* and *epazote* in a bowl. Stuff the chiles with about ½ cup of cheese, press the opening together tightly, and dust with seasoned flour.

2. In a bowl, beat the egg whites until stiff; in a separate bowl, beat the yolks slightly with a pinch of salt and gently fold the yolks into the whites to make the batter.

3. Pour enough oil or melt enough lard in a large skillet to measure 1 inch and heat over medium-high heat until the oil registers 375°F on an instant-read thermometer.

4. Dip the chiles in the batter and fry until golden, 2 to 3 minutes on each side, turning to color both sides. While they are frying, carefully spoon some of the hot oil over the parts of the chiles along the sides that may not be directly touching the oil so they get cooked evenly. Remove and drain on paper towels.

MEXICAN HOT DOGS

PERROS CALIENTES

Yield: Serves 10

I remember eating my first bacon-wrapped hot dog in the '80s as a teenager when we visited Tijuana. Crisp, thin-sliced bacon wrapped around a sizzling TJ Dog, nestled inside a warm tortilla, topped with melted cheese and pickled jalapeños, paired with ice-cold Mexican Coca-Cola made with cane sugar in a glass bottle is street-food heaven! Buy good quality hot dogs for best results (we use Kobe beef in the restaurant), but really any kind works.

1 cup Tomato-*Chile de Árbol* Salsa (recipe follows)

10 hot dogs

3 ounces sharp cheddar cheese

½ cup canned or jarred pickled *jalapeños*

20 slices thin-sliced smoked bacon

10 (8-inch) flour tortillas, warmed, or hot dog rolls

1. Prepare the Tomato-*Chile de Árbol* Salsa (recipe follows).

2. With a sharp knife, cut the hot dogs open lengthwise, making a 2 ½-inch-long slit, leaving the ends intact.

3. Using a vegetable peeler, peel the cheese into strips. Divide the cheese among the hot dogs. Add 2 or 3 jalapeño slices to each, wrap in two slices of bacon, and secure with toothpicks.

4. If grilling, heat your barbecue to medium-hot and warm the tortillas. Wrap the tortillas in foil and put them in a preheated 350°F oven or toaster oven for 10 minutes, or place them directly on the griddle or grill and cook until lightly browned on each side, about 1 minute, turning once.

5. Place the hot dogs on the grill cut side up. When the cheese melts, rotate the hot dogs 15 to 25 degrees to cook each side, about 8 minutes. If broiling, position the rack about 4 inches from the heat and cook for about 8 minutes. Remove with tongs, place each in a warm tortilla or roll, remove the toothpicks, top with Tomato-*Chile de Árbol* salsa, and, if using tortilla, roll up.

ROASTED TOMATO-
CHILE DE ÁRBOL SALSA

Yield: 2 quarts

4 ripe plum tomatoes (about 1 pound)

2 medium unpeeled garlic cloves

1 medium white onion

1 *serrano* chile

1 *chile de árbol*, stemmed and seeded

1 teaspoon freshly squeezed lime juice

1 bunch fresh cilantro, coarse stems removed

Salt

Preheat the broiler. Position a broiler rack 8 inches from the heat. Broil the tomatoes, garlic, onion, and *serrano* and *árbol* chiles until blackened all over. Leave the blackened skin on the vegetables. Transfer all ingredients to the jar of an electric blender and pulse until coarsely chopped; season to taste with salt.

PORK TACOS
CARNITAS TACOS

Serve 8

8 pounds lard

4 pounds pork butts, cut into pieces

10 bay leaves

2 sprigs fresh thyme

2 tablespoons whole peppercorns

1 large stick *canela* (Mexican cinnamon)

1 cup orange juice

1 cup Coca-Cola

1 (8-ounce) can condensed milk

Serrano Salsa (page 19)

Salt

Warm corn tortillas

Shredded cabbage, for garnish

Cilantro leaves, for garnish

Carnitas, which translates as "little meats," have a lot of flavor. These "little" chunks of pork are crisp on the outside and meltingly tender on the inside. My secret ingredient is Coca-Cola, which is a great meat tenderizer and used commonly for this purpose in Mexico. Take the time to make homemade tortillas for these tacos; there is nothing better.

1. Preheat the oven to 350°F.

2. In a large, oven-safe dish, melt the lard over medium-high heat. Add the pork, bay leaves, thyme, peppercorns, *canela*, orange juice, Cola-Cola, and condensed milk; bring to a simmer. Carefully transfer to the oven and cook 1 to 2 hours, or until tender.

3. While the pork cooks, prepare the *Serrano* Salsa.

4. Remove the dish from the oven and heat over medium-high heat on top of the stove to brown the pieces of meat. Season to taste with salt.

5. Cool the meat slightly and shred the larger pieces of meat.

6. Toast each tortilla in a nonstick pan over medium heat for about 30 seconds on each side. Wrap the tortillas in a towel to keep warm. Place the meat onto the warm tortillas, top with a little shredded cabbage and cilantro leaves, and drizzle with *Serrano* Salsa.

PORK SHANK TACOS

TACOS DE CHAMORRO

Yield: Serves 6

12 cloves garlic

4 tomatillos, husked

2 medium white onions, coarsely chopped

4 tablespoons olive or vegetable oil, divided

Salt and freshly ground black pepper

12 black peppercorns

6 bay leaves

2 cloves

2 pieces star anise

2 teaspoons dried oregano, preferably Mexican

2 teaspoons cumin seeds, toasted

6 dried *ancho* chiles, stems and seeds removed, toasted

6 dried *guajillo* chiles, stems and seeds removed, toasted

1 cup apple cider vinegar

1 cup orange juice

3 or 4 large fresh banana leaves

5 medium-size bone-in pork shanks

2 cups chicken stock

Serrano Salsa (page 19)

1 cup Pickled Red Cabbage (page 85)

12 (4-inch) tortillas, warmed

1 cup *queso fresco*, to garnish

Serve your guests a platter of these meltingly tender, perfectly spiced pork shank tacos and you will all swoon with pleasure. Although the ingredient list is long, it's really a simple recipe that produces sweet-tasting, succulent morsels of pork. Cooking the meat on the bone makes a big difference in the taste and texture. I first had them at El Bosque, in Mexico City. It's a true cantina because women aren't allowed in the bar and only in the dining room if accompanied by a man. I went there with Mexican friends who urged me to try the special house cocktail, a "you-LEEP." When it arrived, I cracked up because I saw that it was a mint julep.

1. Preheat the oven to 400°F.

2. Toss the garlic, tomatillos, and onions with 1 tablespoon of oil and season with salt and pepper; spread on a baking sheet and roast until lightly browned, about 15 minutes, turning occasionally. Set aside.

3. Grind the peppercorns, bay leaves, cloves, anise, oregano, and cumin in a *molcajete*, clean coffee mill, or spice grinder.

4. In a medium-size saucepan, cover the toasted chiles with water and bring to a simmer; remove the pan from the heat and set aside for a few minutes to cool. Combine the tomatillo mixture with the chiles, vinegar, and orange juice in the jar of an electric blender and purée until smooth; transfer to a bowl, stir in the peppercorn-bay leaf mixture, and set aside.

5. Line a large roasting pan with banana leaves or parchment paper. Season the pork shanks generously with salt and pepper, rub liberally with the adobo marinade, lay them in the pan, and marinate for at least 1 hour or overnight. Pour the remaining adobo over the top.

6. Preheat the oven to 350°F.

7. Before cooking, return the meat to room temperature, about 45 minutes. Pour in the chicken stock. Fold the banana leaves over the meat, cover with aluminum foil, and seal on all sides; bake until the meat is fork tender and pulling away from the bone, 2 to 3 hours. (If the bones have been removed, the cooking time will be shorter.)

8. While the pork cooks, prepare the *Serrano* Salsa and Pickled Red Cabbage.

9. Remove the meat from the oven, transfer it to a bowl, and let it cool until the meat can be pulled from the bones in medium-size pieces. Pour the cooking liquid through a fine strainer into a bowl and skim the fat from the surface.

10. Heat a tablespoon of the remaining oil in a large skillet over medium-high heat. Add the pork pieces and brown on all sides, turning often, adding more oil as necessary. Ladle about 1 cup of the cooking liquid onto the meat to moisten. Serve hot with crumbled *queso fresco*, plenty of warm tortillas, *Serrano* Salsa, and Pickled Red Cabbage.

BEEF-STUFFED FAT TACOS

GORDITAS DE RES

Yield: Serves 3 to 4

1 cup Tamarind Braised Short Ribs (page 191)

Habanero Salsa II (page 23)

2 cups blue cornmeal

¼ cup all-purpose flour

1 teaspoon baking powder

1 teaspoon salt

1 ½ cups water

Vegetable oil, for frying

¼ cup crumbled *Cotija* cheese

½ cup thinly sliced red cabbage

Gorditas, or "little fat ones," are like thick griddled tacos. While usually filled with stewed meats like beef, pork, or chicken, they can be made simply with black beans and/or cheese or seafood. In Mexico's Lake Pátzcuaro area—mystically known as the place where the barrier between life and death is the thinnest—they are made with blue corn.

1. Prepare the Tamarind Braised Short Ribs and *Habanero* Salsa.

2. In a large bowl, mix the cornmeal and all-purpose flour, baking powder, and salt together; add the water and stir until the dough is smooth. Form the dough into walnut-size balls, cover, and set aside.

3. Moisten a cloth napkin and spread it out on a flat surface. Roll each ball of dough in the moistened palms of your hands until smooth, press your thumb into the center of each ball to make a dimple, and fill it with a tablespoon of braised short ribs. Roll again to cover the short ribs and put the balls on the napkin. Cover each ball with a plastic bag and press down to flatten it into a ½-inch disk.

5. Fill a large cast iron skillet about halfway up with oil and heat over medium-high heat to 375°F when measured on an instant-read thermometer. Slide a few patties into the hot oil and fry until light golden brown and crispy, about 1 minute per side. Don't crowd. Remove with a slotted spoon or tongs and drain on paper towels. As soon as they are cool enough to handle, make a slit on the side of each disk and stuff with 1 teaspoon crumbled cheese and a little cabbage; drizzle with 1 teaspoon of *Habanero* Salsa and serve.

SHEPHERD-STYLE TACOS

TACOS AL PASTOR

Yield: Serve 8 to 12

Shepherd's style cooking is said to have originated with Lebanese immigrants to the city of Puebla, many of whom tended flocks. Lamb, a favorite Mediterranean meat, was originally cooked on the spit, but eventually other meat, including pork, was used. Whereas Mexicans traditionally season dishes with chiles, this recipe includes ground black pepper, reflecting another Eastern influence. The recipe makes a generous amount—each person can enjoy two or three tacos—so it's a great dish for a street party.

40 dried *guajillo* chiles

20 dried *ancho* chiles

20 dried *pasilla negro* chiles

2 ½ cups freshly squeezed orange juice

Grated zest of 1 orange

⅓ cup firmly packed dark brown sugar

9 cloves garlic

1 ½ tablespoons cumin seeds, toasted and ground

1 ½ tablespoons kosher salt

1 tablespoon freshly ground black pepper

1 tablespoon dried oregano, preferably Mexican

8 ounces Mexican beer

6 ounces cola

1 ½ tablespoons white vinegar

1 tablespoon freshly squeezed lime juice

4 pounds pork shoulder, trimmed and cut into ½-inch cubes

Roasted Pineapple-*Pasilla de Oaxaca* Salsa (recipe follows)

3 tablespoons vegetable oil

1 small pineapple, peeled, cored, and cut into ½-inch-thick slices, for garnish

24 (4-inch) soft white corn tortillas

1. Stem and seed the *guajillo, ancho,* and *pasilla negro* chiles; combine them in a stainless steel bowl with just enough hot water to cover, weigh them down with a plate, soak until soft, 15 to 20 minutes, then drain and set aside. Reserve the soaking liquid.

2. In a small saucepan, simmer the orange juice over medium-low heat until reduced by half. Set aside. In the jar of an electric blender, purée the softened chiles until smooth, adding some of the soaking water, if needed, to get a smooth consistency.

3. In a large bowl, combine the reduced orange juice, puréed chiles, orange zest, brown sugar, garlic, cumin, salt, black pepper, and oregano. Stir in the beer, cola, vinegar, and lime juice. Add the pork, turning to coat evenly, cover, refrigerate, and marinate overnight.

4. Prepare the Roasted Pineapple-*Pasilla de Oaxaca* Salsa (at right).

5. When ready to cook, drain the pork well and blot the pieces dry with paper towels. In a large, heavy skillet, heat the oil over medium-high heat. Sauté the pork, in batches if necessary so as not to crowd the pan, until the meat is cooked through, about 10 minutes, turning to cook evenly. Remove from heat

and serve right away, or keep warm in the pan over low heat until ready to serve.

6. While the pork is cooking, heat a gas grill or skillet over high heat. Add the pineapple and cook until lightly browned, turn, and cook the second side until lightly colored. Remove and cut into cubes.

7. To serve: on a large platter, lay the tortillas side by side, overlapping them slightly. Divide the filling among them; top with grilled pineapple and Roasted Pineapple-*Pasilla de Oaxaca* Salsa and serve.

ROASTED PINEAPPLE-*PASILLA DE OAXACA* SALSA

Yield: 3 ½ cups

1 ¼ pounds tomatillos, husked, rinsed, and quartered

2 teaspoons lard or vegetable oil

5 medium cloves garlic

7 small *pasilla de Oaxaca* chiles

½ pineapple, peeled, cored, and sliced

Salt

1. In a small saucepan, cover the tomatillos with enough water to come about halfway up the side of the pan, cover, and cook over medium heat until the tomatillos are soft, about 10 minutes; strain, reserving the liquid.

2. Meanwhile, on the plancha or in a heavy skillet over medium high heat, melt the lard, add the garlic, and cook until soft and well charred on all sides, 5 to 10 minutes. Add the chiles and toast for 2 minutes per side; tear them into pieces, discarding the stem, and transfer them to the jar of an electric blender.

3. Either under the broiler, on a gas grill, or in the skillet, grill the pineapple until well caramelized, turning once. Transfer it to the jar of the blender along with enough of the chile rehydrating liquid to make the blades turn smoothly, add a large pinch of salt, and blend until smooth. Add the tomatillos and blend; season to taste with salt.

MEATBALLS IN CHIPOTLE SAUCE

ALBONDIGAS EN SALSA DE CHIPOTLE

Yield: Serves 6 to 8

Are these the best meatballs anywhere? I certainly think they rank right up there with some of the finest versions in Mexico. They're very meaty and the combination of beef, pork, and veal gives them a rich flavor. A friend of my mom's from Milan, who was a wonderful cook, taught me how to make meatballs and I use her secret recipe along with a few secrets of my own. Meatballs around the world are a popular comfort food and are often served in broth or soup in Mexico.

Chipotle Salsa (recipe follows)

1 cup chicken stock

10 cloves garlic, coarsely chopped

1 large white onion, coarsely chopped

1 bunch flat-leaf parsley, chopped (reserve a few chopped leaves for garnish)

1 pound ground beef

1 pound ground pork

1 pound ground veal

5 large eggs, lightly beaten

1 cup grated *Cotija* cheese, or substitute Romano, plus ½ cup more for garnish

¼ cup dried breadcrumbs

¼ cup chile powder

1 tablespoon cumin seeds, toasted and ground

1 teaspoon crushed red pepper flakes

1 tablespoon salt

1. Make the *Chipotle* Salsa.

2. While the salsa is simmering, prepare the meatballs: In the jar of an electric blender, combine the chicken stock with the garlic, onion, and parsley and purée until smooth.

3. In a large bowl, combine the beef, pork, and veal with the eggs, *Cotija* cheese, breadcrumbs, chile powder, cumin, red pepper flakes, and salt. Add the chicken stock mixture and gently mix until just combined; form into walnut-size meatballs.

4. Heat the remaining oil in a large casserole, add the meatballs, and brown evenly on all sides; add the *Chipotle* Salsa, bring to a simmer, and cook until the meatballs are cooked through, about 15 minutes. Serve over rice or pasta with grated *Cotija* cheese and the remaining chopped fresh parsley.

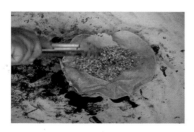

CHIPOTLE SALSA

1 large white onion

Olive or vegetable oil

4 cloves garlic

1 (28-ounce) can peeled tomatoes including juices

2 canned *chipotles en adobo*

1 bay leaf

1 teaspoon cumin seeds, toasted and ground

1 teaspoon *epazote*, or substitute fresh basil

1 teaspoon dried oregano, preferably Mexican

1 teaspoon ground cinnamon, preferably *canela* (Mexican cinnamon)

½ teaspoon freshly ground black pepper

⅛ teaspoon ground allspice

Salt to taste

1. Turn the broiler on. Lightly brush the onion with a little oil and broil it in a flat pan about 5 inches from the heat until soft and golden, turning once.

2. In a small skillet, heat a few drops of oil over medium heat; add the garlic and sauté until soft and golden, shaking the pan occasionally. Transfer the onion and garlic to the jar of an electric blender; add the tomatoes, *chipotles*, bay leaf, cumin, *epazote*, oregano, cinnamon, pepper, and allspice and purée until smooth. Pour the mixture into a large saucepan and simmer for 30 minutes; season to taste with salt.

BEEF, BLACK BEAN, AND CHORIZO CHILI

CHILI CON CARNE, FRIJOLES NEGROS Y CHORIZO

Yield: Serves 6 to 8

2 (3-ounce) links Mexican chorizo, casing removed and thinly sliced

1 ½ pounds beef stew meat, cut into 1-inch cubes

1 ½ cups chopped white onion

4 cloves garlic, minced

4 canned *chipotles en adobo*, chopped

3 tablespoons tomato paste

2 teaspoons sugar

2 teaspoons unsweetened cocoa

1 teaspoon ground coriander

1 teaspoon ground cumin

1 teaspoon dried oregano, preferably Mexican

2 to 3 teaspoons salt

1 (28-ounce) can whole tomatoes including juice, chopped

4 cups beef or chicken stock

1 cup dry red wine

¼ cup freshly squeezed lime juice

2 tablespoons *masa harina* dissolved in 2 tablespoons warm water

2 (15-ounce) cans pinto beans, rinsed and drained

1 (15-ounce) can black beans, rinsed and drained

There are chili heads everywhere, but in Colorado, their numbers are great. And while there are countless versions of chili stew in Mexico and the American West, the unsweetened cocoa powder here imparts a depth of flavor to which most chilis can only aspire. Serve it with tortillas, chopped onion, grated cheese, avocados, and pickled jalapeños . . . or go crazy with any topping you like!

1. Heat a large heavy casserole over medium-high heat, add the chorizo, and sauté until browned, about 3 minutes, breaking it into pieces with a wooden spatula; remove with a slotted spoon. Add half of the beef to the pan and brown on all sides, about 5 minutes. Remove and repeat with the remaining beef. Stir in the onion and garlic and sauté for 3 minutes.

2. Return the chorizo and beef to the pan along with the chiles, tomato paste, sugar, cocoa, coriander, cumin, oregano, and salt; cook for 1 minute, stirring constantly. Add the tomatoes, stock, wine, and lime juice and bring to a boil; reduce the heat and simmer for 1 hour, stirring occasionally.

3. Gradually stir in the *masa harina*. Add pinto beans and black beans and bring to a boil, cover, reduce the heat, and simmer for 30 minutes.

SAUSAGE (STEP BY STEP)

OAXACAN CHICHILO

CHICHILO OAXAQUEÑO

Yield: Serves 4 to 6

During the time I spent in Oaxaca studying their famous seven moles, I attended classes with Susana Trilling, the passionate owner-chef-teacher of Seasons of My Heart Cooking School. Few moles are as complex and seductive as chichilo, my favorite of these sauces, known as the legendary "seventh mole" that is traditionally served for festivals and feasts. While complex, dark, and smoky in flavor, this robust beef and vegetable stew isn't overly spicy but it's definitely not light on the tongue.

1 ½ pounds meaty beef bones or short ribs

2 quarts water

8 cloves garlic, chopped, plus 1 additional clove

2 carrots, peeled and chopped

2 stalks celery, chopped

1 white onion, chopped, plus 1 additional small onion

5 whole black peppercorns

1 bay leaf

3 whole allspice berries, divided

1 *chile de árbol* or substitute 1 large *piquin* or *santaka* chile

2 cloves, divided

½ pound pork butt, cut in 1-inch cubes

6 *guajillo* chiles, stems and seeds removed, seeds reserved, or substitute dried red New Mexican chiles

5 *chilhuacle negro* chiles, stems and seeds removed, seeds reserved, or substitute *ancho* chiles

1 corn tortilla, torn into strips

1 sprig fresh oregano

1 sprig fresh thyme

1 teaspoon cumin seeds

1 (2-inch) stick *canela* (Mexican cinnamon)

4 large tomatoes, quartered

3 fresh tomatillos, husked and halved

5 small potatoes, peeled and quartered

2 chayotes or substitute 2 zucchini, thinly sliced

½ pound green beans, cut in 1-inch lengths

3 tablespoons lard or vegetable oil

2 to 3 avocado leaves, toasted

Salt to taste

Sliced onions, to garnish

Lime slices, to garnish

1. In a large stockpot, cover the bones with cold water, bring to a boil, and cook for 20 minutes, skimming off any foam that rises to the top. Lower the heat, add 1 clove of garlic, the carrots, celery, white onion, peppercorns, bay leaf, 1 allspice berry, the *chile de árbol*, and 1 clove; sauté for 5 minutes. Add the pork, lower the heat, and simmer, covered, for 1 hour. Strain the liquid into a large bowl, refrigerate until cool, and skim off any fat that forms on the top. Discard the solids.

2. In a large frying pan or comal, toast the *guajillo* and *chilhuacle negro* chiles until darkened but not burned, turning once. Transfer them to a bowl, cover with hot water, and soak for ½ hour to soften.

3. Meanwhile, toast the tortilla strips on the comal or in the skillet until blackened; remove. Toast the reserved chile seeds until the seeds are blackened; remove and put in bowl with water to soak. After 5 minutes, change the water, soak for 5 more minutes, and drain.

4. Drain the chiles and transfer them to the jar of an electric blender along with the tortillas, blackened seeds, oregano, thyme, remaining allspice, remaining clove, cumin, and cinnamon; add a little water and purée into a paste. Set aside.

5. Roast the tomatoes and tomatillos on the comal until soft and remove. Roast the remaining onion and garlic cloves. Transfer them all to the blender and purée.

6. Bring 3 cups of the reserved stock to a boil and add the potatoes, chayote, and beans; reduce the heat and simmer until the potatoes are easily pierced with a fork. Drain and reserve the vegetables.

7. Heat the lard or oil in a heavy pot or cazuela over medium-high heat; add the chile purée and fry for a few minutes. Stir in the tomato mixture and fry for a couple of minutes more. Stir in just enough beef stock to thin the mixture. Add the avocado leaves, purée the mixture in the blender, in batches if necessary, and pass through a large strainer; season to taste with salt.

THIS MOLE IS UNIQUE IN THAT THE CHILE SEEDS AND TORTILLA ARE IGNITED ON A COMAL OR IN A PAN UNTIL VERY, VERY DARK AND THEN GROUND INTO THE SAUCE. LIKE ALL MOLES, IT'S ALL ABOUT THE SAUCE, SO IT'S USUALLY SERVED IN WIDE, FLAT SOUP BOWLS WITH PLENTY OF TORTILLAS.

CHILHUACLE NEGRO CHILES ARE THIN-SKINNED, BULBOUS BLACK CHILES WITH A DEEP EARTHY FLAVOR THAT ISN'T ESPECIALLY HOT. THE CHILES ARE RARELY FOUND OUTSIDE OF OAXACA. ALTHOUGH THEY GROW WILD IN THAT REGION, THEY HAVE BECOME SO RARE THAT EVEN LOCALS ARE FORCED TO SUBSTITUTE OTHER CHILES.

ISTHMIAN-STYLE MEATLOAF

PASTEL DE CARNE DEL ISTMO

Yield: Serves 10

Throughout the Yucatán, this meatloaf is sold in stands or carts at markets and at velas, or fiestas. Often it's served at room temperature, so it's perfect as a sandwich or quick bite on the street. I discovered they do some pretty weird stuff there, like using animal crackers and deviled ham in their mole sauce. In other dishes, like Camarones Aguachile (page 123), they use vitamin C tablets to make it bright green.

½ cup blanched almonds

4 ounces slab bacon, or 2 to 3 thick slices, cut into ⅓-inch cubes

4 ounces boiled ham, cut into ½-inch cubes

4 ounces smoked Mexican chorizo, finely chopped

3 cloves garlic, minced

1 large white onion, finely chopped

2 cups Japanese (panko) breadcrumbs

1 (5-ounce) can evaporated milk

1 pound ground pork

1 pound ground beef

1 large egg, lightly beaten

1 (3 ½-ounce) can deviled ham

2 red bell peppers, roasted, peeled and finely chopped

2 canned *chipotles en adobo* (page 272), minced

½ cup pimiento-stuffed green olives, finely chopped

3 tablespoons mayonnaise

3 tablespoons minced flat-leaf parsley leaves

2 tablespoons sliced pickled *jalapeños*, thinly sliced

1 tablespoon Dijon mustard

1. Preheat the oven to 350°F.

2. Spread the almonds on a baking sheet and toast until fragrant and lightly browned, 10 to 15 minutes; remove, chop coarsely, and set aside.

3. In a heavy, medium-size skillet, combine the bacon with 2 tablespoons of water and cook over medium-high heat for 5 minutes, stirring frequently, until the water has evaporated and some of the fat has been rendered. With a slotted spoon, remove the bacon and set aside.

4. Strain the fat from the first pan (which will have a salty residue at the bottom) into a large skillet set over medium-high heat. Add the partly cooked bacon along with the ham and sausage. Cook until lightly browned, about 3 minutes, stirring frequently.

5. Using a slotted spoon or spatula, transfer the meat mixture to a bowl, leaving as much fat as possible in the pan. Discard all but about 2 tablespoons of fat. Add the garlic and onion and sauté over medium-high heat until the onion is translucent, about 5 minutes, stirring often. Add to the meat mixture.

6. Meanwhile, in a medium-size bowl, combine the breadcrumbs and evaporated milk; let stand for 5 to 10 minutes to absorb the liquid while the meat mixture cools slightly.

7. In a large bowl, lightly mix the pork and beef with the soaked breadcrumbs and beaten egg. Add the deviled ham, pimientos, *chipotles*, olives, mayonnaise, parsley, *jalapeños*, and mustard and mix thoroughly with your hands. Shape the mixture into two 9-inch loaves and place on a baking sheet or a rack set in a roasting pan. (Alternatively, you can pack the mixture firmly into two 9 x 5-inch loaf pans.) Bake until golden brown, about 1 hour, and serve hot or (as in the Isthmus) at room temperature.

 COOKING TIP

IF DESIRED, THE MEAT MIXTURE MAY BE PREPARED AHEAD AND REFRIGERATED FOR 3 TO 4 HOURS, THEN RETURNED TO ROOM TEMPERATURE AND BAKED IN THE OVEN. I MADE THIS RECENTLY FOR AN APPEARANCE AT THE JAMES BEARD HOUSE, IN NEW YORK, CELEBRATING THE IRRESISTIBLY UNIQUE ISTHMIAN CUISINE.

BACON TAQUITOS WITH ROASTED TOMATO REMOULADE

TAQUITOS DE TOCINO

Yield: Serves 4 as an *antojito* (appetizer)

Roasted Tomato Remoulade (recipe follows)
2 pounds thick sliced smoked bacon
1 white onion, finely diced
¼ cup honey
2 tablespoons *ancho* chile powder
1 teaspoon *chipotle* chile powder
Salt
Vegetable oil, for deep-frying
8 corn tortillas
Thinly sliced radishes, to garnish
Shaved lettuce, to garnish

These bacon taco bites are close to being a perfect food. They taste at once crunchy, smoky, and earthy as the flavors combine in each mouthful. They are great for a lazy Sunday breakfast with eggs and a Bloody Maria. Or serve them for Super Bowl, Cinco de Mayo, or any fiesta in the 'hood.

1. Prepare the Roasted Tomato Remoulade.

2. In a large skillet, cook the bacon over medium heat until crisp; remove to paper towels to drain. Reserve the fat in the pan. Cut the bacon crosswise into 1-inch strips and put in a bowl.

3. In the same skillet, sauté the onions until golden brown. Using a slotted spoon, transfer the onions to the bowl with the bacon, add the honey and *ancho* and *chipotle* powders, and season to taste with salt.

4. Fill a deep fat fryer with oil or add enough oil to a deep skillet to measure about 1 inch deep and heat to 375°F on an instant-read thermometer.

5. Roll about 2 tablespoons of the filling mixture in each corn tortilla, secure with 2 toothpicks, and deep-fry until golden brown and crispy. Remove, drain on paper towel, discard the toothpicks, and serve with Roasted Tomato Remoulade, radishes, and shaved lettuce.

ROASTED TOMATO REMOULADE

Yield: 2 cups

2 plum tomatoes, split lengthwise

1 egg yolk, at room temperature

2 teaspoons freshly squeezed lemon juice

½ teaspoon Dijon mustard

½ teaspoon rice vinegar

½ cup vegetable oil

1 teaspoon smoked hot paprika, such as *pimentón de la Vera*

1 teaspoon chopped tarragon leaves

Salt and freshly ground pepper

1. Preheat the oven to 200°F.

2. Roast the tomatoes on a sheet pan, cut side down, for 15 to 20 minutes, or until dry; coarsely chop and set aside.

3. In a food processor, combine the egg yolk, lemon juice, mustard, and vinegar and process for 1 minute. With the motor running, slowly drizzle in the oil, beginning with a drop at a time and gradually increasing the flow as the mixture emulsifies. Add the tomatoes, paprika, and tarragon and pulse until combined but not completely smooth; season to taste with salt and pepper. Scrape into a bowl and set aside.

MEXICAN RIBEYE SHISH KABOB WITH MEXICAN RISOTTO

FILETE DE LOMO AL ALAMBRES Y ARROZ CON CREMA

Yield: Serves 6

2 cloves garlic
1 *serrano* chile
¼ cup Maggi sauce (page 273)
¼ cup cilantro leaves
2 tablespoons freshly squeezed lime juice
½ teaspoon kosher salt
½ teaspoon freshly ground black pepper
½ cup olive oil, plus a little more oil for the skillet, if not cast-iron
3 pounds (1 ½-inch-thick) ribeye steak, trimmed
Arroz con Crema, optional (recipe follows)
12 strips thick-sliced smoked bacon, cut in half crosswise
18 cipollini onions, blanched in boiling water and blotted dry
18 cremini mushrooms
4 *poblano* chiles, seeded and cut into 1 ½-inch squares
Arbol Chile Salsita (recipe follows)
Pico de Gallo (page 18), for garnish
Warm tortillas
6 (12-inch) metal skewers

When Mexicans do kabobs, the results are full of bravado. In this version, cubes of ribeye steak are wrapped in bacon and skewered along with cipolini onions, cremini mushrooms, and poblano chiles on metal skewers or alambres, a word that means "wire" in Mexican Spanish. At Dos Caminos, we serve these with Arbol Chile Salsita and Pico de Gallo over Arroz con Crema.

1. In the jar of an electric blender, combine the garlic, *serrano* chile, Maggi sauce, cilantro, lime juice, salt, and pepper and purée until smooth. With the motor running on medium speed, slowly pour in the oil and blend until incorporated. Transfer the marinade to a bowl or large resealable plastic bag, add the meat, and marinate for at least 2 hours, but preferably overnight in the refrigerator.

2. Prepare the *Arroz con Crema.*

3. Preheat the oven to 350°F.

4. Pat the meat dry on paper towels. Heat a large cast-iron or other heavy skillet over high heat until hot, brushing lightly with oil, if needed. Sear the steak for 2 to 3 minutes per side, remove, and let cool; cut into 1 ½-inch cubes.

5. Cook the bacon on a baking sheet in the oven until cooked but not crisp, about 7 minutes. Wrap each cube of steak with a half strip of bacon. Thread the beef and vegetables onto the skewers. Season with salt and pepper, refrigerate.

6. Make the *Arbol* Chile Salsita and the *Pico de Gallo.*

7. Heat a barbecue, gas grill, or broiler until hot. Position the rack about 5 inches from the heat and grill for about 3 minutes per side, cooking all 4 sides, and then spoon about 2 tablespoons of the *Arbol* Chile Salsita on top of each, and drizzle with 2 tablespoons of *Pico de Gallo.*

8. Serve Kebob with warm tortillas and *Arroz con Crema.*

ARROZ CON CREMA
MEXICAN RISOTTO WITH ROASTED CORN, POBLANO CHILES, AND CILANTRO

Yield: Serves 6

This creamy side dish is a willing partner for all grilled and broiled meat, poultry, and fish dishes. We serve it with our ribeye alambres (Filete de Lomo al Alambres). Chihuahua cheese comes from the Mexican state of the same name.

4 cups cooked long grain white rice, such as Uncle Ben's

Kernels from 2 ears grilled corn cut from the cob (about 1 ½ cups)

1 cup heavy cream

2 to 3 *poblano* chiles, roasted, peeled, and cut into small cubes

½ cup grated *queso Chihuahua* or grated Monterey Jack cheese

¼ cup grated *Cotija* cheese

¼ cup chopped cilantro leaves

Kosher salt

In a medium-size saucepan over medium heat, combine the rice, corn, cream, and *poblano* chiles and simmer until the mixture binds together, stirring frequently. Add the *Chihuahua* and *Cotija* cheeses and stir until creamy; stir in cilantro, season to taste with salt, and serve warm.

ARBOL CHILE SALSITA

Yield: 1 cup

2 tablespoons chopped garlic

2 to 4 *chiles de árbol*, toasted and crushed, or 1 to 2 tablespoons crushed red pepper flakes, according to taste

¼ cup sherry vinegar

2 tablespoons Maggi sauce

2 tablespoons freshly squeezed lime juice

¼ cup chopped cilantro leaves

Kosher salt and freshly ground black pepper

In a bowl, stir together the garlic, *árbol* chile, vinegar, Maggi sauce, and lime juice; add the cilantro and season to taste with salt and pepper.

CHILE AND BEER BRAISED BRISKET

ESTOFA DE CARNE DE RES EN BIERA

Yield: Serves 4

6 *ancho* chiles, stemmed, seeded, and torn into 1-inch pieces
1 pound roasted and diced tomatoes
4 cloves garlic, coarsely chopped
1 large onion, coarsely chopped
1 tablespoon *árbol* chile powder
2 teaspoons ground cumin
1 teaspoon salt
1 cup Mexican beer, such as Negra Modelo
1 tablespoon vegetable oil
2 pounds flat cut brisket, trimmed

Use this brisket for Machacado Tacos con Huevos (page 52) as a hearty breakfast, or for delicious enchiladas or tamales. In Mexico it's unheard-of to serve meat like this without a tortilla in some form. It's either served on top of a tortilla, with sopas, or served on the side for making tacos.

1. Preheat the oven to 350°F.

2. In a large bowl, cover the chiles with hot water and soak until softened, at least 20 minutes. Drain.

3. Combine the tomatoes and their juices, garlic, onion, chile powder, cumin, salt, and drained chile pieces in the container of a food processor and process until smooth. Scrape into a large bowl and stir in the beer.

4. In a large roasting pan, heat the oil over medium heat; add the brisket and brown on all sides, about 6 minutes total cooking time. Pour the chile sauce over the meat and bring to a simmer, cover, transfer to the oven, and braise until the meat is fall-apart tender, 2 ½ to 3 hours.

5. Transfer the meat to a cutting board and pull it apart into long shreds using two forks. Stir the shredded meat back into the sauce. Serve in an enchilada or a taco.

TAMARIND BRAISED SHORT RIBS

ESTOFA DE COSTILLAS CORTAS EN TAMARINDO

Yield: Serves 8

8 beef short ribs, about 6 to 8 pounds
4 tablespoons kosher salt
6 *chiles de árbol*
1 large white onion, diced
1 large carrot, diced
1 bay leaf
1 cup balsamic vinegar
1 cup dry white wine
½ cup firmly packed dark brown sugar
1 tablespoon chopped garlic
1 cup tamarind paste
1 cup hot water
Salt and freshly ground black pepper

Short ribs are another cut of beef that lends itself to long, slow braising to develop mouthwatering flavors as the meat fibers break down and become meltingly tender. I serve them at Dos Caminos with Elote de la Calle (page 103) and tortillas for diners to make their own tacos.

1. Heat the oven to 350°F.

2. Season the short ribs generously with kosher salt. Lay them side by side in a large heavy roasting pan. Scatter the *chiles de árbol*, onion, carrot, and bay leaf on top of the meat.

3. In a small bowl, stir together the vinegar, wine, brown sugar, and garlic and pour over the short ribs. In a separate bowl, whisk the tamarind paste and hot water together to dissolve it a little; combine with the vinegar-wine liquid and pour into the pan. The liquid should come about three-quarters of the way up the sides of the short ribs. Add more water, if necessary.

4. Cover the pan tightly with foil and again with a second layer of foil. Transfer the pan to the oven and braise the ribs until the meat falls apart when poked with a fork, 3 to 3 ½ hours, removing the foil to check that it is tender. Carefully remove the ribs to a platter, cover, and set aside at room temperature.

5. Strain the liquid through a fine strainer into a large container. Chill for at least 1 hour so the fat rises to the top and forms a solid chunk; remove and discard.

6. In a large, deep skillet over high heat, bring the braising liquid to a boil and reduce to about 4 cups; return the short ribs to the pan, reduce the heat to medium-low, and simmer until the ribs start to be glazed with the sauce, turning them with a pair of tongs so they become glazed and sticky, 20 to 25 minutes. Keep warm. Remove from the heat, pull the meat off the bones, and tear into large chunks.

MOLE SHORT RIBS

ESTOFA DE COSTILLAS CORTAS EN MOLE NEGRO

Yield: Serves 8

In little stalls along the markets, vendors sell takeaway plates of short ribs, most often over mashed sweet potatoes or Puré de Boniato con Mojo (page 101). You can read my diary entry about learning to make Mole Negro with Abigail Mendoza on page 36.

1 recipe *Estofa de Costillas Cortas en Tamarindo* (page 191)

Mole Negro (page 34)

Puré de Boniato con Mojo (page 101)

Espinacas con Pepitas y Pasas (page 107)

Tri-Color Rajas (page 25)

1. Cook the short ribs according to the recipe on page 191 and leave whole. Prepare the *Mole Negro*, *Puré de Boniato con Mojo*, *Espinacas con Pepitas y Pasas*, and Tri-Color Rajas.

2. To serve, remove the bones and cut each into three equal pieces, cover with 2 cups of *Mole Negro*, and reheat. Ladle ½ cup of *Mole Negro* in a pool in the center of the serving bowl(s).

3. For each serving, spoon ½ cup *Puré de Boniato* in the center of the *mole*, and add ½ cup *Espinacas con Pepitas y Pasas* next to it. Arrange the short ribs in a pinwheel on top of the sweet potatoes and spinach. Top with Tri-Color Rajas.

RED WINE-ANCHO BRAISED BEEF CHEEKS

CACHETES EN VINO ROJO

Yield: Serves 4

4 tablespoons vegetable oil, divided

4 (12-ounce) beef cheeks, trimmed of excess fat

Salt and freshly ground black pepper

1 medium white onion, finely chopped

1 carrot, finely chopped

½ stalk celery, finely chopped

1 tablespoon Szechwan peppercorns

½ teaspoon unsweetened cocoa powder

2 cups hearty red wine

8 *ancho* chiles, stemmed and seeded

3 cups canned whole tomatoes including juice, chopped

Tortillas (about 3 per person)

> YOU CAN ALSO USE THE MIXTURE TO FILL ENCHILADAS OR TAMALES, OR IT'S ESPECIALLY GOOD OVER RICE.

Mexicans, like Europeans and many other cultures, cook and eat all parts of the animal. Braised beef cheeks are particularly rich and succulent. For this dish, I took a typical Mexican-style recipe and "Frenchified" it. What you get are incredibly moist mouthfuls of beef that you can serve with tortillas to make tacos.

1. Heat 2 tablespoons of the oil in a large-heavy pot over medium-high heat until hot but not smoking. While the oil is heating, pat the beef cheeks dry and season with salt and pepper.

2. Add as many pieces of beef to the pan as will fit comfortably without crowding and brown on all sides, about 20 minutes total; using tongs, transfer the pieces to a bowl. Once all the pieces are browned, pour off the fat, add the remaining 2 tablespoons oil along with the onion, carrot, celery, and peppercorns and cook over medium-low heat until softened, about 10 minutes, stirring occasionally.

3. Meanwhile, heat the oven to 325°F.

4. Stir the cocoa powder into the vegetable mixture, pour in the wine, and scrape up any browned cooking bits. Increase the heat to high and boil until the liquid is reduced by half, about 10 minutes. Return the cheeks along with any juices to pot; add the *ancho* chiles and tomatoes, and season with salt and pepper to taste. Bring to a simmer, cover, transfer to the middle of the oven, and cook until very tender, about 3 hours.

5. Remove the pot from oven. Carefully remove the meat and, when cool enough to handle, shred into a bowl. Pass the vegetables and liquid through a fine strainer, pressing to extract as much liquid as possible, and return the liquid back to the pan. Discard the vegetables. Warm the meat in the liquid and serve with tortillas.

SPICY CHERRY GLAZED BABY BACK RIBS

COSTILLAS EN SALSA DE CEREZAS PICANTE

Yield: Serves 6 to 12

Banana leaves

6 racks baby back ribs, rinsed in cold water and patted dry

1 bunch thyme, stemmed and finely chopped

1 bunch oregano, stemmed and finely chopped

½ bunch rosemary, stemmed and finely chopped

2 cups sliced shallots

½ cup sliced garlic

6 bay leaves

1 tablespoon whole allspice berries

1 tablespoon ground cumin

1 tablespoon ground coriander

2 tablespoons *achiote* paste

5 lemons, sliced

5 limes, sliced

3 cups orange juice

Spicy Cherry Glaze (recipe follows)

Toasted sesame seeds, to garnish

If we were in Mexico, these tender Yucatán-style baby back ribs might well be wrapped in leaves and cooked in a deep pit. Barring a hole in your backyard, the ribs are encased in traditional banana leaves, covered with spices and orange juice, and slowly baked with a zesty cherry glaze. Spareribs are a great icebreaker and add a fiesta-like atmosphere to any dining event.

1. Preheat the oven to 350˚F. Arrange the banana leaves in the bottom of a deep 21 x 13-inch or other pan large enough so the ribs will be completely covered.

2. In a bowl, combine the thyme, oregano, rosemary, shallots, garlic, bay leaves, allspice, cumin, coriander, and *achiote* paste. Lay the ribs in the pan and distribute the seasoning mixture evenly over them. Add the lemons and limes, pour the orange juice over the meat, cover the pan with foil, seal tightly, and bake until tender, about 1 ½ hours. Remove from the oven, leave the pan covered, and cool the ribs to room temperature.

3. While the ribs cook, prepare the Spicy Cherry Glaze (at right).

4. Generously coat the ribs with the glaze. Heat the broiler and position the rack about 5 inches from the heat. Broil for 10 minutes to crisp the glaze; sprinkle on the sesame seeds and serve immediately.

SPICY CHERRY GLAZE
Yield: 3 cups

1 tablespoon vegetable oil
3 cups frozen sour cherries, defrosted
1 cup diced red onion
4 tablespoons minced fresh ginger
2 tablespoons minced garlic
4 tablespoons soy sauce
3 tablespoons Sriracha hot sauce
2 tablespoons reposado tequila
1 tablespoon sherry wine vinegar
1 teaspoon sesame oil
Salt and pepper to taste

1. In a medium-size skillet over medium heat, combine the oil, cherries, onion, ginger, and garlic sauté until the onions are lightly browned.

2. Stir in the soy sauce, hot sauce, tequila, vinegar, and sesame oil and simmer for 15 minutes; season with salt and pepper to taste.

OXTAIL TAMALES IN MOLE DE XICO

TAMALES DE RABO DE BUEY EN MOLE DE XICO

Yield: Serves 4 to 6 (12 tamales)

2 tablespoons olive oil

6 pounds oxtails, cut into 2- to 3-inch pieces, seasoned with salt and pepper

½ cup diced Mexican chorizo

4 cloves garlic, chopped

2 carrots, diced

1 white onion, diced

1 bay leaf

½ teaspoon smoked hot paprika, such as *Pimentón de la Vera*

1 cup dry white wine

2 pounds plum tomatoes, charred, seeded, peeled, and puréed

2 tablespoons chopped cilantro

2 tablespoons chopped flat-leaf parsley

1 tablespoon sherry vinegar

2 cups *Mole de Xico* (page 41)

2 cups *masa harina*

3 ounces lard

1 cup chicken stock, or more, as needed

1 tablespoon salt

Banana leaves cut into 12 (6 x 6-inch) squares

Crema, to garnish

Toasted sesame seeds, to garnish

I'm going to say up front that this is a complicated mole recipe. There are several ingredients and it takes all day. But the tamales are well worth the effort and you'll be patting yourself on the back. You can do the prep for this in stages over a couple of days.

1. Heat the oil in a large, heavy pan over medium-high heat. Add as many pieces of oxtail as will fit comfortably in the bottom without crowding and brown on both sides; remove and continue with the remaining pieces.

2. Preheat the oven to 350°F.

3. Stir in the chorizo, garlic, carrots, and onions and sauté until wilted. Add the bay leaf and paprika; pour in the wine, and scrape up any browned cooking bits. Stir in the tomato purée and simmer for 2 to 3 minutes; add the cilantro, parsley, and vinegar. Return the oxtails to the pot, cover, and transfer to the oven to braise until tender, 3 to 3 ½ hours, turning the oxtails once. Remove from the oven and cool the oxtails in the liquid.

4. Meanwhile, prepare the *Mole de Xico* and *masa*. For the *masa*: In the bowl of a stand mixer, combine the *masa harina* and lard and beat until light. Add the stock and salt and beat until you have a smooth dough.

5. When the oxtails are tender, remove, cool, and shred the meat with your hands or two forks.

6. Assemble the tamales: For each banana leaf square, spoon on about 2 tablespoons of *masa* and spread into a 4-inch oval shape. Add 1 tablespoon of filling, fold up the bottom halfway, and fold in the two sides to form triangles. Steam the tamales as per the recipe on page 98; remove and serve covered with the *Mole de Xico* sauce and drizzled with crema and sesame seeds.

On the Mole Trail in Xico

The town of Xico, in the state of Veracruz, is an enchanting place reached by traveling through fragrant coffee fields that is renowned throughout the country for its *mole de Xico*. Because the region grows a lot of fruits, including citrus and berries that are used for local medicinal liqueurs and cure-alls, their dark, thick *mole* includes a higher percentage of dried fruits, including prunes, plantains, and apples, than most other *moles*, so it is sweeter and also nuttier. On page 41, you'll find my version of the one served on the lovely patio at El Mezón Xiqueño with their squawking *guacamayas*, or macaws, and beautiful indoor greenhouse.

SLOWLY BRAISED LAMB

BARBACOA DE BORREGO

Yield: Serves 6 to 8

6 *guajillo* chiles, stemmed and seeded

12 allspice berries

¼ cup dried oregano, preferably Mexican

2 teaspoons ground cumin

6 cloves garlic

1 white onion, chopped

2 tablespoons fresh thyme leaves

⅓ cup cider vinegar

6 pounds lamb shoulder

Salt and freshly ground black pepper

3 banana leaves

6 avocado leaves

This fragrant, tender lamb dish is my present-day take on lamb barbacoa, one of Mexico's oldest and most well-known dishes. Traditionally, the meat is wrapped in avocado and/or banana leaves and slowly cooked in a pit for several hours or even overnight until it becomes succulent and tender. Ours is rubbed with chile paste and then cooked in a slow oven for about 4 ½ hours.

1. In a large casserole, bring 2 quarts of water to a boil. Meanwhile, toast the chiles on both sides on a heated griddle or in a skillet until fragrant, about 5 minutes. Transfer to a bowl, cover with boiling water, and let stand for 20 minutes; drain and add to the jar of an electric blender.

2. Grind the allspice, oregano, and cumin in a *molcajete*, clean coffee mill, or spice grinder; add them to the blender along with the garlic, onion, thyme, vinegar, and ½ cup water.

3. Score the skin of the lamb with ½-inch deep cuts; season with plenty of salt and pepper.

4. Line a large roasting pan first with banana leaves, then top with avocado leaves. Put the meat into the pan and rub the chile paste all over the lamb. Wrap the leaves around the meat, cover the pan tightly with plastic wrap, and refrigerate overnight.

5. Heat the oven to 300°F.

6. Remove the plastic wrap and roast the lamb until it is very tender and falling off the bone, about 4 ½ to 5 hours, turning once about halfway through. Pour the juices into a bowl and skim off the fat. Shred the meat. Pour the juices back over the meat and toss to combine.

BARBACOA DE BORREGO (STEP BY STEP)

BABY GOAT STEW

BIRRIA DE CHIVO

Yield: Serves 4

4 *guajillo* chiles

3 *ancho* chiles

3 *cascabel* chiles

2 tablespoons cider vinegar

1 teaspoon salt

1 teaspoon freshly ground black pepper

1 teaspoon oregano, preferably Mexican

½ teaspoon ground thyme

¼ teaspoon cinnamon

¼ teaspoon cloves

¼ teaspoon ground cumin

5 pounds bone-in baby goat, cut in large chunks

6 cloves garlic, finely diced

2 bay leaves

1 large white onion, coarsely chopped, plus 1 cup chopped onion, for garnish

1 cup chopped cilantro, for garnish

Corn tortillas

Goat is less familiar to most Americans than beef, lamb, or pork, but hopefully this aromatic casserole cooked in typical Mexican style will open your eyes to delightful-tasting meat. The meat is marinated overnight in a spiced chile mixture then cooked on a rack that sits over simmering water in a tightly covered pot. As the meat steams, it becomes moist, flavorful, and tender.

1. In a hot pan, toast the *guajillo*, *ancho*, and *cascabel* chiles until browned but not burned. Remove the seeds and veins; cover the chiles with hot water and soak until softened, 15 to 20 minutes. Transfer them to the jar of an electric blender and process with the vinegar into a paste.

2. Mix the salt, pepper, oregano, thyme, cinnamon, clove, and cumin in a bowl. Rub the goat liberally with the mixture and then coat the meat with half of the chile paste. Set the meat in a shallow dish, cover, and marinate overnight in the refrigerator.

3. Preheat your oven to 350°F.

4. Fill a large, deep roasting pan halfway up with water. Add the garlic, bay leaf, 1 chopped onion, and any remaining marinade. Place the meat on a rack that sits just above the water, cover with foil, and bake for 4 hours.

5. Remove the meat and discard the bones; chop the meat into large chunks and set aside. Remove the bay leaves from the liquid. If needed, reduce the liquid in a small pan to a gravy consistency. Spoon it over the meat and turn to coat the chunks with the remaining chile sauce; serve with the remaining chopped onion, cilantro, and tortillas on the side.

BEEF TONGUE IN FRESH RED SALSA

LENGUA EN SALSA ROJA CRUDA

Yield: Serves 4 to 6

In Mexico, sliced, cubed tongue is a popular taco filling. It's also a favorite of my buddy Scott Linquist, my best friend and co-executive chef at Dos Caminos. The sweet meat marries well with the lively, acidic taste of the serrano chiles and tomatoes. Use plenty of warm tortillas.

3 to 4 pounds beef tongue, trimmed of excess fat

12 peppercorns

6 cloves garlic

1 white onion, coarsely chopped

6 sprigs thyme

6 sprigs fresh marjoram

2 bay leaves

¼ cup kosher salt

Salsa Roja Cruda (recipe follows)

Corn tortillas, warmed

1. In a large saucepan, cover the tongue with cold water; add the peppercorns, garlic, onion, thyme, marjoram, bay leaves, and salt and bring to a boil over high heat. Adjust the heat down and simmer until the meat is tender, about 3 hours.

2. Meanwhile, prepare the *Salsa Roja Cruda* (below).

3. Cool the tongue in the broth; peel it and return it to the broth to cool completely. When cold, slice the tongue into bite-size pieces and serve with *Salsa Roja Cruda*.

SALSA ROJA CRUDA

Yield: 2 quarts

1 pound Roma or plum tomatoes, seeded and finely chopped

1 ¼ cups finely chopped white onion

¾ cup chopped cilantro

5 *serrano* chiles, seeded and finely chopped

Kosher salt

In a nonreactive bowl, combine the tomatoes, onion, cilantro, and chiles; season to taste with salt.

RABBIT IN ADOBO

CONEJO EN ADOBO

Yield: Serves 6

Mexicans are fond of rabbits, especially since they are readily available. This dish makes me think about springtime, especially with the ramps that are just pushing up from the ground at this time of the year. (Scallions may be substituted.) The delicate meat is wonderful in enchiladas. Cut-up rabbits are available at many butchers. If you buy whole rabbits, you could roast the loins and serve them sliced alongside this dish, if desired.

Hind and front quarters from 5 rabbits
10 peppercorns
3 cloves garlic
3 bay leaves
1 white onion, coarsely chopped
Adobo Sauce (recipe follows)
Pickled Ramps (recipe follows)

1. Combine the rabbits, peppercorns, garlic, bay leaves, and onions in a large saucepan, cover with cold water, and bring to a boil; adjust the heat down and simmer for 1 hour.

2. Meanwhile, prepare the Adobo Sauce and Pickled Ramps (right).

3. Cool the rabbit in the liquid; remove, pull the meat from the bones in large pieces, and reserve in a bowl. Reduce the broth by half, stir in the Adobo Sauce, and strain over the meat; heat and serve with Pickled Ramps on the side.

ADOBO SAUCE

Yield: 1 cup

5 *pasilla* chiles, seeds and membranes removed
3 *ancho* chiles, seeds and membranes removed
3 cloves garlic, coarsely chopped
3 black peppercorns, crushed
3 sprigs fresh thyme
3 sprigs marjoram
3 whole cloves, crushed
½ stick *canela* (cinnamon), crushed
¼ teaspoon cumin seeds, crushed
1 tablespoon white vinegar

In a large bowl, soak the *pasilla* and *ancho* chiles in hot water to cover for 10 minutes; using a slotted spoon, transfer them to the jar of an electric blender, add ½ cup of the chile rehydrating water, and purée. Add the garlic, peppercorns, thyme, marjoram, cloves, *canela*, cumin, and vinegar and purée until smooth.

PICKLED RAMPS

Yield: Serves 6 to 8

1 pound fresh ramps or scallions, trimmed and lightly blanched in salted water
¾ cup water
¾ cup sugar
¾ cup rice wine vinegar
1 tablespoon kosher salt
½ teaspoon crushed red pepper
½ teaspoon *ancho* chile powder

Put the ramps or scallions in a heatproof bowl. In a small saucepan, combine the water, sugar, vinegar, salt, red pepper, and chile powder and bring to a boil. When the sugar dissolves, pour the liquid over the ramps, cover, and refrigerate overnight.

DESSERTS/POSTRES

STRAWBERRIES AND CREAM

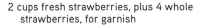

FRESAS CON CREMA

Yield: Serves 4

2 cups fresh strawberries, plus 4 whole strawberries, for garnish

1 tablespoon granulated sugar

1 cup heavy cream or 1 (7.6-ounce) can Media *Crema* (see page 273)

½ cup whole milk

⅓ cup confectioners' sugar

Whipped cream, for garnish

All over Mexico, vendors sell takeaway cups of luscious fresh strawberries and cream as well as other fresh fruits and ice creams. Often, you find a combination of strawberries and peaches.

1. Slice the strawberries, sprinkle them with granulated sugar, and set aside.

2. In a medium-size bowl, beat the heavy cream or Media table cream, milk, and confectioners' sugar with a whisk into soft peaks.

3. Spoon the strawberries into parfait glasses, about 1 cup per person. Pour the cream over the berries and top with whipped cream and a whole strawberry.

Chef Margarita Carillo

After breakfast at the hotel, we went back to El Centro Culinario Ambrosía for a *mole* class with Chef Margarita Carillo, of Don Emilia restaurant, in Los Cabos. This was by far the most outstanding class for me, as Margarita is a great teacher with an incredible depth of knowledge about the origins of Mexican cuisine, and I learned a lot.

Among this dishes we made, there was a delicious *Sopa Oaxaca de Camaron* with dried shrimp, an interesting beet *mole*, a wonderful hazelnut and pistachio *mole*, and a dessert of prickly pear with anise. (Check out my recipes for Prickly Pear Vinaigrette and Prickly Pear and Celery Agua Fresca on pages 76 and 241.) After lunch at the school, we moved on to dessert class, where we prepared *ate de guayaba*, guava paste made with fresh guavas and an amazing condiment for fresh cheese; a sweet tomatillo marmalade; peanut marzipan; and a fantastic fruit dessert, Candied Papaya scented with fig leaf (page 209).

Dinner was at *Azul y Oro*, the restaurant of the National University of Mexico, with Chef Ricardo Muñoz, a very famous cookbook author and authority on the foods of Veracruz with whom I have taken classes in the past. He prepared a dinner of Veracruz specialties, including *guanabana horchata*, *Arroz a la Tumbada* (page 139), pulpos en su tinto, and hot chocolate *atole*.

CANDIED PAPAYA

DULCE DE LECHOSA

Yield: Serves 8

Candied papaya is a beloved dessert that I learned to make with Baja chef Margarita Carillo at a seminar for professional chefs at El Centro Culinario Ambrosía in Mexico City. It's wonderful when served with queso fresco.

1 medium (about 3 pounds) Mexican papaya, peeled, seeded, and cut into ½-inch slices

3 cups sugar

½ teaspoon salt

2 tablespoons freshly squeezed and strained lime juice

1 (2-inch) stick *canela* (Mexican cinnamon)

1 fig leaf

1. Lay the papaya in a single layer in a large heatproof casserole. Add the sugar and salt, and then drizzle on the lime juice and enough water to barely cover the papaya.

2. Add the cinnamon stick and fig leaf; bring to a simmer and cook very gently, partially covered, until the papaya starts to look translucent, about 1 hour. Remove from the heat and cool.

CANDIED PUMPKIN

CALABAZA EN TACHA

Yield: 2 ½ quarts

The Day of the Dead (page 64) is a major celebration in Mexico when family members honor their ancestors. Candied pumpkin is a classic dessert to serve for that holiday and it is also put on traditional altars.

1 (2 ½ pound) pumpkin

6 tablespoons unsalted butter

2 tablespoons ground cinnamon, preferably *canela* (Mexican cinnamon)

1 tablespoon vanilla extract

⅓ cup firmly packed light brown sugar

4 pieces star anise

1 pound *piloncillo*, chopped

1. Preheat the oven to 375°F.

2. Cut the pumpkin in half, remove the skin and seeds, and cut the flesh into ½-inch squares.

3. In a saucepan, combine the butter, cinnamon, vanilla, and brown sugar; cook over medium heat, stirring occasionally, until the butter is completely melted and becomes caramel syrup. Remove the pan from the heat, pour the caramel on the pumpkin, add star anise, and stir to coat the pumpkin with the syrup.

4. Scrape into a large baking dish and sprinkle the *piloncillo* on top. Cover with aluminum foil and bake in the center of the oven for 25 minutes; remove the foil and bake for another 10 minutes. Remove and serve warm or chilled.

DOS CAMINOS
MEXICAN STREET FOOD

JAMONCILLO
MEXICAN MILK FUDGE

Yield: 16 squares

This milky fudge-like candy is among my favorite Mexican indulgences. There are Latino grocery stores that sell it, but I always ask friends to bring me some when they come north of the border. Yet, as the recipe shows, it's really very easy to make.

Butter to grease the pan
1 quart whole milk
1 ¾ cups sugar
2 teaspoons pure vanilla extract
1 teaspoon baking soda
1 (4-inch) stick *canela* (Mexican cinnamon)
1 cup chopped pecans
16 pecan halves, for garnish

1. Butter a 9 x 9-inch square pan.

2. In a large, heavy saucepan, combine the milk, sugar, vanilla, baking soda, and *canela* and bring to a boil over medium heat. Using a candy thermometer, cook until the mixture reaches the softball stage, 240˚F, at least 20 minutes.

3. Remove from the heat, take out the cinnamon stick, and add the chopped pecans. Beat with a hand held mixer for about 5 minutes at medium speed, being careful to avoid splatters. Pour the candy into the pan, press the pecan halves onto the top of the warm candy for decoration, and let cool; cut into 16 pieces. Store the candy in an airtight container for up to 2 weeks.

MEXICAN DONUTS FILLED WITH SPICED COFFEE CREAM

CHURROS CON CREMA DE CAFÉ DE OLLA

Yield: Serves 8

Finely grated zest of 2 oranges

2 cups water

1 cup unsalted butter

3 tablespoons plus ½ cup sugar

1 teaspoon salt

2 cups all-purpose flour

8 large eggs

Crema de Café de Olla (recipe follows)

2 quarts vegetable oil, for frying

1 tablespoon ground cinnamon, preferably *canela* (Mexican cinnamon)

Dos Caminos guests adore our Mexican doughnuts. The light, airy churros (see sidebar) are filled with a luscious, spiced coffee cream filling. This recipe is easily doubled to feed a great crowd of friends who, we assure you, won't be able to stop celebrating two Mexican treasures: Oaxaca's cinnamon-scented chocolate (page 247) and crunchy, fried churros.

1. Line a sheet pan with parchment.

2. In a saucepan, combine the orange zest, water, butter, 3 tablespoons sugar, and salt and bring to a rolling boil over high heat. Using a whisk, quickly stir in the flour all at once. Reduce the heat to medium and continue stirring until all of the ingredients are well incorporated and the dough is smooth.

3. Transfer the dough to an electric stand mixer fitted with the paddle attachment and start beating on medium speed. Add the eggs one at a time as the dough cools; continue beating 5 minutes longer or until the eggs are well incorporated.

4. Fill a pastry bag fitted with a wide star tip with the dough and pipe it onto the sheet pan in strips measuring 3 inches long and 1 inch wide. Freeze until firm on the edges, about 10 minutes, so they can be handled more easily. Meanwhile, make the *Crema de Café de Olla*.

5. In a deep pot, heat the oil to 375°F as measured on an instant-read thermometer. Fry the churros until golden brown, about 2 minutes. Do not crowd. Remove with a slotted spoon to a plate lined with paper towels to cool. Push a channel through both ends of each churro with the handle of a wooden spoon.

 CHURROS

CHURROS ORIGINATED IN SPAIN CENTURIES AGO, BUT AFTER THE CONQUEST, THEY QUICKLY SPREAD TO MEXICO AND ARGENTINA. THE SHORT, RIDGED STICKS OF FRIED DOUGH ARE MOST FREQUENTLY EATEN FOR BREAKFAST WITH A CUP OF THICK HOT CHOCOLATE. SOME MEXICAN CHURROS (LIKE THOSE ABOVE) ARE LONGER AND FILLED WITH CUSTARD.

6. Fill a pastry bag with the *Crema de Café de Olla* and pipe it into the churros; refrigerate for 30 minutes to set. (They can be made up to 2 hours ahead.)

CREMA DE CAFÉ DE OLLA
SPICED COFFEE CREAM

3 tablespoons grated *piloncillo*
2 tablespoons all-purpose flour
2 cups whole milk
½ vanilla bean, split and scraped
1 (4-inch) stick *canela* (Mexican cinnamon)
4 whole cloves
1 (2-inch x ½-inch) piece orange zest
3 large eggs, lightly beaten
2 tablespoons unsalted butter
1 ½ teaspoons instant espresso powder
1 ½ teaspoons sugar

1. Combine the *piloncillo* and flour in a medium-size bowl.

2. In a heavy saucepan, combine the milk, vanilla bean, *canela*, cloves, and orange zest; heat over medium-high heat until small bubbles form at the edge of the pan.

3 Whisk ½ cup of the hot milk into the sugar-flour mixture until smooth; then return the sugar mixture to the saucepan.

4. In a separate bowl, whisk the eggs with ½ cup of the hot milk mixture. Stir it back into the heated milk mixture and cook over medium heat until thickened. Remove from the heat and, using a fine strainer, strain the liquid into a mixing bowl; whisk in the espresso powder and granulated sugar. Cool completely before filling the churros.

5. Dust with cinnamon and serve.

COCONUT RICE PUDDING EMPANADAS

EMPANADAS DE PLÁTANOS CON ARROZ CON LECHE DE COCO

Yield: Serves 4

Georgina Sanchez, a prep cook from Oaxaca, first made these turnovers for me when I was working at Ciudad, Mary Sue Milliken and Susan Feniger's Pan-Latin popular restaurant in Los Angeles. I've never forgotten her for this wonderful gift and have enjoyed them many times since in the Mercado 20 de Noviembre, in Oaxaca City.

Rice Pudding (recipe follows)
3 ripe plantains, unpeeled
1 ripe banana, peeled
1 teaspoon salt
All-purpose flour, for dusting hands
¼ cup vegetable oil
Confectioners' sugar, for garnish
Crème fraîche, for garnish

1. Prepare the Rice Pudding (recipe follows).

2. While the pudding is cooling, preheat the oven to 350°F.

3. Cut a lengthwise slit in each plantain and put them on a baking sheet; bake until the flesh is thoroughly soft and oozing, 40 to 50 minutes, then set aside to cool.

4. Using a food processor or electric stand mixer fitted with a paddle attachment, make the dough. Peel, trim, and discard any tough ends from the plantains. If the plantains are too moist, spread them on a baking sheet and put in a 250°F oven to dry, about 15 minutes.

5. Combine the plantains, banana, and salt in the food processor and pulse until a smooth purée is formed, or mix by hand until just blended, being careful not to overwork the dough or it will become too starchy. Cover with plastic wrap and chill for about 2 hours.

6. To assemble the empanadas, dust your hands with a little flour; roll 2 tablespoons of the dough lightly between your palms to form a ball. Line the bottom of a tortilla press with a small plastic bag and place the ball of dough in the center. Put another small bag over the dough and press to form a 3 ½-inch circle.

7. Spoon about 1 teaspoon of the Rice Pudding on half of each dough circle, fold the other half over to enclose it, and press the edges together to seal. Put the empanadas on a platter and chill for at least 30 minutes, or for up to a day. (Stuffed empanadas can also be frozen for up to six months and cooked later.)

8. To cook the empanadas, heat the oil in a medium skillet over medium-high heat. Fry 4 to 6 empanadas, at a time, shaking the pan constantly, for about 1 minute per side or until they are dark brown all over. Remove with a slotted spoon and drain on paper towels. Serve hot, dusted with confectioners' sugar and with *crème fraîche* for dipping.

RICE PUDDING

1 cup jasmine rice

1 (13 ½-ounce) can coconut milk

1 ¼ cups whole milk

½ cup sugar

Finely grated zest of 1 lime

2 tablespoons shredded coconut, lightly toasted

In a medium bowl, soak the rice for 20 minutes in enough water to cover. Drain and transfer to a heavy 3-quart saucepan. Stir in the coconut milk, whole milk, and sugar and bring to a boil. Reduce the heat and simmer uncovered until thickened, about 25 minutes, stirring occasionally. Remove the pan from the heat, stir in the lime zest and coconut, and chill.

DOS CAMINOS
MEXICAN STREET FOOD

CRÊPES WITH GOAT'S MILK CARAMEL

CREPAS DE CAJETA

Yield: Serves 8 (16 crêpes)

CREPAS

2 quarts goat's milk

1 ½ cups sugar

1 tablespoon vanilla extract

1 quart vanilla ice cream

CAJETA

Yield: 16 crêpes

¼ cup cake flour

¼ unbleached all-purpose flour

¼ cup ground pistachios

2 teaspoons sugar

½ teaspoon salt

1 ¼ cups whole milk

4 tablespoons (¼ cup) melted butter

1 tablespoon brandy

2 large eggs, plus 1 large egg yolk

Cajeta is often confused with dulce de leche, the Argentine caramel made with cow's milk, while the more intricate, deeply flavored cajeta is made with goat's milk. The name comes from a small balsa-wood box, or cajita, specially made to store the caramel before refrigeration was widespread. Homemade cajeta is infinitely superior to store-bought versions except in the case of the old-fashioned Dulcería de Celaya, in Mexico City, where they have been selling sweets since 1874, including their world-famous cajeta.

1. In a large bowl, mix both flours, the pistachios, sugar, and salt together.

2. In a small saucepan, heat the milk, butter, and brandy over medium-high heat until warm.

3. Stir the eggs into the dry ingredients and whisk in the milk-butter mixture; chill for at least 8 hours or overnight.

4. Meanwhile, prepare the *cajeta*: In a large saucepan, bring the goat's milk, sugar, and vanilla to a simmer; reduce the mixture over low heat until the milk turns caramel brown and coats the back of a spoon, about 1 hour.

5. Heat an 8-inch nonstick skillet. Ladle in a generous ⅓ cup of the *crepas* batter, rotating the pan in order to cover the bottom. Cook until the edges are lightly browned, about 2 minutes, then turn and cook the second side for the same amount of time. Transfer the crêpe to a plate, and cover with a damp towel and inverted plate to keep warm while finishing the other crêpes.

6. Serve each guest 2 warm crêpes folded in quarters with ¼ cup of the sauce spooned over the top with a scoop of vanilla ice cream.

DARK CHOCOLATE ANCHO CHILE CARAMEL CUSTARD

FLAN DE CHOCOLATE

Yield: Serves 8

1 cup sugar

¼ cup water

1 tablespoon espresso powder

4 ounces dark chocolate, chopped

1 cup skim milk

½ tablespoon *ancho* chile powder

1 cup, plus 2 tablespoons evaporated milk

1 cup condensed milk

3 large eggs

This dessert is among the most beloved desserts in Mexico . . . and the world. It is creamy and smooth with notes of espresso and ancho chile powder. Use the best-quality chocolate you can find for this contemporary version.

1. Preheat the oven to 325°F.

2. In a small saucepan, cook the sugar and water over high heat until the mixture turns rich, dark amber, 5 to 7 minutes, stirring occasionally; add the espresso powder and mix until well blended. Remove the pan from the heat and immediately pour the caramel into an 8-inch round cake pan and swirl to cover the bottom. Alternatively, use 8 individual ramekins. Set aside to cool while preparing the custard.

3. Put the chocolate in a medium mixing bowl. In a medium saucepan, bring the skim milk and *ancho* chile powder to a boil; remove from the heat, cover with plastic wrap, and let it infuse for 10 minutes. While still hot, strain it over the dark chocolate, stirring until the chocolate is melted. Let cool.

4. In a large container, combine the cooled milk-chocolate mixture with the evaporated milk, condensed milk, and eggs. Using a handheld or immersion blender, mix until thoroughly combined. Strain through a very fine strainer or very fine cheesecloth into a bowl.

5. Put the cake pan or ramekins in a deep baking pan and fill with enough warm water to come three-quarters of the way up the sides. Fill the cake pan or ramekins with the flan mixture, cover the pan with aluminum foil (being careful not to let the foil to touch the top of the flan), and pierce in several places to create vents.

6. Bake for about 30 minutes (or 15 minutes for the ramekins); then very carefully lift off the corner of the foil to allow the steam to escape. Recover the cake pan or ramekins and continue to bake until the flans are set around the edges but still slightly loose in the center, about 10 to 15 minutes longer for the large pan or 5 to 10 minutes for the ramekins.

7. Remove from the oven; lift the cake pan or ramekins from the water and transfer to a cooling rack. Cool to room temperature, then cover, and refrigerate overnight. To unmold the flan, run a small knife around the sides of the cake pan or ramekins and invert onto a platter or individual dessert plates.

FRITTERS
BUÑUELOS

Yield: Serves 8

3 cups all-purpose flour, sifted

2 tablespoons sugar, plus ½ cup sugar for coating

1 teaspoon kosher salt

½ teaspoon baking powder

2 large eggs, beaten

¼ cup whole milk

3 tablespoons lard or solid vegetable shortening

3 tablespoons unsalted butter, softened

1 vanilla bean or 1 teaspoon vanilla extract, to drizzle

1 cup honey, to drizzle or dip

1 teaspoon cinnamon, for coating

4 cups vegetable oil, for frying

Puffed, crispy, golden fritters are a staple at Christmastime and at every carnival throughout Mexico. Our version, drizzled with vanilla-infused honey and cinnamon sugar, is always a popular sweet.

1. In a bowl, sift together the flour, 2 tablespoons of sugar, salt, and baking powder. In the center of the bowl, add the eggs, milk, shortening, and butter and mix to form a ball.

2. Turn the dough out onto a lightly floured board and knead until smooth, adding more flour or milk by the tablespoon, as needed. Cut the dough into four equal pieces, cover each with plastic wrap, and refrigerate for at least 30 minutes.

3. Cut the vanilla bean in half lengthwise, scraping out the pulp and seeds from the center of the bean; combine with the honey in a small saucepan and warm over low heat to about 165°F; let it steep while making the *buñuelos*.

3. In a small bowl, combine the remaining ½ cup of sugar with the cinnamon. Cut each piece of dough into 12 equal pieces and roll them into balls. On a lightly floured board, flatten each ball into a disc about ¼ inch thick; then press your thumb into the center of each disc to form a well.

4. In a large, deep skillet, add enough oil to measure at least 1 ½ inches deep; heat to 350°F on an instant-read thermometer. Add the *buñuelos* in batches and fry until golden brown, turning once. Remove with a slotted spoon and drain on paper towels. Remove the vanilla bean from the honey. Quickly toss the *buñuelos* in cinnamon sugar, drizzle with honey, and serve hot.

MELON AND CUCUMBER FRUIT POPS

PALETAS DE MELÓN Y PEPINO

Yield: 8 ice pops

1 medium cantaloupe or ½ honeydew melon, peeled and coarsely chopped

½ hothouse cucumber, peeled, seeded, and coarsely chopped

1 *jalapeño*, stem and seeds removed, coarsely chopped

½ cup sugar, or to taste

1 lime, cut into wedges

These icy, spicy Mexican pops from Michoacan aren't the beloved "Otter Pops" from my childhood. (But I still like those, too!) They can be both rustic and sophisticated and are made in a hypnotizing array of colors and flavors, including creamy mamey, cajeta, hibiscus, guanabana, and the frozen heat of pepino or mango con chile. They are a favorite of children and adults alike.

In the jar of an electric blender, purée the melon, cucumber, and *jalapeño* until smooth. Add sugar to taste. Fill 8 ice pop molds with the mixture, transfer them to the freezer, and freeze until solid, about 6 hours. Serve each with a slice of lime.

DOS CAMINOS
MEXICAN STREET FOOD

STRAWBERRY AND LYCHEE SHAVED ICE WITH TROPICAL FRUIT CEVICHE

RASPADO DE FRESAS Y LICHIS

Yield: Serves 4

1 pint fresh strawberries, stemmed and hulled

1 pint fresh lychees, peeled and seeded or 1 (12-ounce) can lychees

1 cup water

1 cup sugar

1 tablespoon freshly squeezed lime juice

Tropical Fruit Ceviche (recipe follows)

1 mango

TROPICAL FRUIT CEVICHE

Yield: about 1 quart

¼ medium pineapple, peeled, cored, and diced

1 small papaya, peeled, seeded, and diced

1 mango, peeled and diced

½ pint strawberries, stemmed and diced

1 cup sugar

2 limes

Mexican raspados taste much better than the snow cones of my youth. Although they are both made with shaved ice, the Mexican version, like this combination of strawberries and lychees, is made only with fresh fruits and sugar, then frozen, and scraped before serving. I like to serve my version with a tropical fruit salad. Raspados can be made two days in advance and kept frozen in a covered container.

1. Make the *raspado*: Combine the strawberries and lychees in the jar of an electric blender and purée until smooth. Add the water, sugar, and lime juice and blend.

2. Transfer the mixture to a shallow metal pan and freeze, stirring and crushing the lumps with a fork every 30 minutes for 2 to 3 hours or until it is firm. Before serving, scrape the *raspado* with a fork to lighten the texture.

3. Prepare the Tropical Fruit Ceviche (below).

4. To assemble: Peel and slice the mango and fan it out in the bottom of 4 glass cups, forming a base or cup. Scoop ¼ cup of the strawberry-lychee *raspado* into the mango base, spoon the Tropical Fruit Ceviche on top of the *raspado*, and serve.

In a medium bowl, combine the pineapple, papaya, mango, and strawberries; add the sugar and toss gently to combine. Using a micro-plane or a box grater, zest the limes. Squeeze the limes and add the juice and zest to the fruit; mix just to combine.

ROSE PETAL ICE CREAM

HELADO DE ROSAS

Yield: 1 quart

If you saw the movie Like Water for Chocolate, based on Laura Esquivel's novel Como agua para chocolate, you will clearly recall the incendiary passions ignited when Pedro eats Tita's quail in rose petal sauce. While I can't promise my rose petal ice cream and cookies will evoke such amorous feelings, I think you'll find it deliciously romantic or romantically delicious. We serve Helado de Rosas with Bizcochos de Rosas for Valentine's Day at Dos Caminos.

2 cups loosely packed, unsprayed rose petals, washed and lightly patted dry (see page 276)

1 cup sugar

1 cup heavy cream

1 cup half-and-half

4 large egg yolks

1 teaspoon vanilla extract

¼ cup rose water

1. Combine the rose petals with the sugar in a food processor and process until the mixture becomes a paste.

2. In a double boiler, combine the heavy cream, half-and-half, and sugar-rose petal mixture and bring to a simmer over medium heat.

3. In a large mixing bowl, whisk the yolks until they are pale yellow; slowly add the cream mixture to the bowl while whisking vigorously. Add the vanilla extract and rose water and whisk until blended.

4. Chill the mixture in the refrigerator or over an ice bath to about 38°F; strain into an ice-cream maker and process according to the manufacturer's directions.

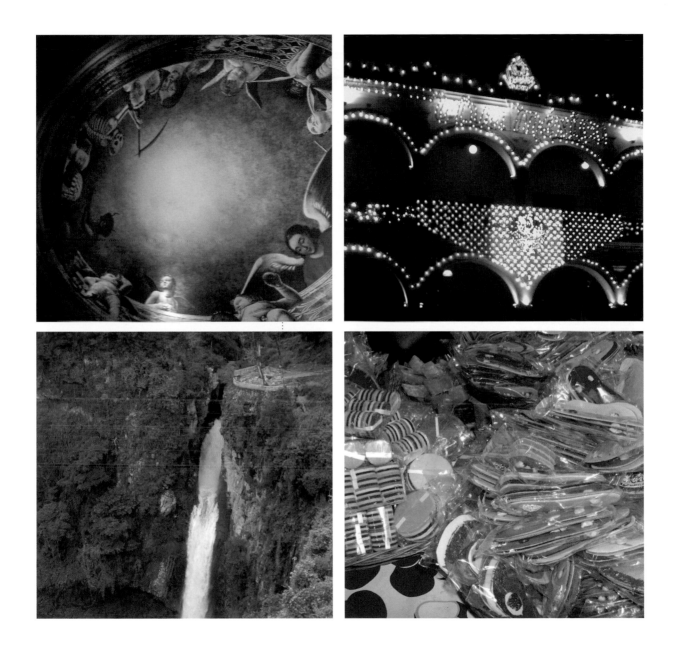

DOS CAMINOS
MEXICAN STREET FOOD

ROSE PETAL COOKIES

BIZCOCHOS DE ROSAS

Yield: 18 cookies

½ cup lard

¾ cup sugar, divided

2 tablespoons rose water

2 tablespoons fresh orange juice

1 large egg yolk

¾ cup unbleached all-purpose flour

½ cup ground dried rose petals

½ teaspoon ground cinnamon, preferably
    canela (Mexican cinnamon)

¼ teaspoon ground cloves

These traditional Mexican cookies should be made with lard to have the right delicately crumbly texture. Don't forego one of the best cookies you will ever eat. A little lard never hurt anyone. I follow Julia Child's philosophy of "everything in moderation." Chefs and home cooks, with updated nutritional information, are discovering that fact.

1. Position a rack in the upper and lower thirds of the oven and preheat the oven to 350°F.

2. In an electric stand mixer fitted with a paddle attachment, whip the lard until it is light and creamy. Beat in ¼ cup sugar, rose water, and orange juice. Beat in the egg yolk and then the flour.

3. Roll the dough out between two sheets of waxed paper to a thickness of ½ inch. Cut out cookies in whatever shapes you like, transferring them to ungreased baking sheets. Bake for 12 to 15 minutes, exchanging the position of the sheets on the racks from top to bottom and from front to back at the halfway point, until the cookies are crisp and lightly colored.

4. For the coating, mix the ground rose petals with the remaining ½ cup of sugar, the cinnamon, and cloves in a wide shallow dish. Carefully dredge the cookies in the spiced sugar while they are warm. Cool completely on a rack and store at room temperature in airtight tins.

PINEAPPLE-LIME SORBET

SORBETE DE PIÑA Y LIMON

Yield: 1 quart

2 cups water

1 ½ cups sugar

7 tablespoons freshly squeezed lime juice, strained and divided

1 ¼ cups unsweetened pineapple juice

2 tablespoons grated lime zest

½ cup grated fresh pineapple

We serve this refreshing sorbet in our Agua de Chilacayota (page 237), but it's great by itself, too.

1. In a medium-size saucepan, combine the water, sugar, and 3 tablespoons of the lime juice and bring to a boil. Reduce the heat and simmer until the sugar dissolves, about 5 minutes. Remove the pan from the heat, put it in an ice bath, and cool completely. Stir in the remaining lime juice, pineapple juice, and lime zest and cool.

2. Pour the mixture into the freezer can of an ice-cream maker and freeze according to the manufacturer's instructions. Scrape the sorbet into a large baking dish and stir in the pineapple; transfer to a container, cover, and freeze completely.

TAMARIND SORBET AND COCONUT ICE CREAM SUNDAE WITH MACADAMIA-CHIPOTLE BRITTLE

SORBETE DE TAMARINDO, HELADO DE COCO Y TURRÓN DE MACADAMIA

Yield: Serves 8

The many delicious components in this sundae—tamarind sorbet and coconut ice cream dressed with rum-brown sugar syrup and macadamia-chipotle brittle—add up to a yummy and intricate dessert. You can prepare them ahead (and even cheat with purchased ice cream) and then assemble the sundae just before serving. When making piloncillo syrup, if the brown sugar cone is grated, as the recipe states, then the 7 to 8 minutes cooking time is correct. However, when it is coarsely chopped, it could take at least 15 minutes over low heat to melt.

TAMARIND SORBET

Yield: 1 quart

1 cup water

½ cup firmly packed light brown sugar

½ cup frozen tamarind pulp, available online or at Asian or Latin markets

1 tablespoon freshly squeezed lemon juice

1. Bring the water and sugar to a simmer in a small saucepan over low heat until the sugar dissolves and simmer for 5 minutes. Remove and pour the syrup into a mixing bowl. Cool to room temperature.

2. Whisk the tamarind pulp and lemon juice into the sugar syrup, then strain.

Pour the mixture into an ice-cream maker and process according to the manufacturer's instructions. Put the sorbet in an airtight container and freeze for at least 2 hours before serving.

COCONUT ICE CREAM

Yield: ½ gallon

1 cup shredded unsweetened coconut
2 cups heavy cream, divided
1 cup whole milk
¾ cup sugar
¼ teaspoon salt
1 vanilla bean, split in half lengthwise
5 large egg yolks
½ teaspoon vanilla extract

1. Preheat the oven to 350°F.

2. Spread the coconut on a sheet pan and bake until golden brown, 3 to 4 minutes, stirring frequently so it toasts evenly and watching that it doesn't burn.

3. In a medium saucepan, warm 1 cup of the heavy cream, the milk, sugar, and salt over low heat; add the toasted coconut and scrape the vanilla seeds into the milk along with the pod. Cover, remove from the heat, and steep for 1 hour at room temperature.

4. Rewarm the coconut-infused mixture. Set a fine strainer over another medium saucepan and strain the mixture into the saucepan.

5. Pour the remaining heavy cream into a large bowl and put a fine strainer on top of it.

6. In a separate medium bowl, whisk the egg yolks until pale yellow in color. Slowly pour the warm coconut-infused mixture into the yolks, whisking vigorously, then return the egg yolks to the saucepan. Stir the mixture constantly over medium heat with a heatproof spatula, scraping the bottom as you stir, until the mixture thickens and coats the spatula, 6 or 7 minutes. Strain the custard into the cream, stir in the vanilla extract, and cool over an ice bath to room temperature. Transfer to the refrigerator and chill thoroughly; transfer to an ice-cream maker and freeze according to the manufacturer's instructions.

RUM-*PILONCILLO* SYRUP

Yield: 2 cups

2 (6-ounce) cones *piloncillo*, grated
1 cup water
¼ cup purchased spiced rum
1 piece star anise
1 (4-inch) stick *canela* (Mexican cinnamon)
1 clove
¼ teaspoon anise seeds

Combine the *piloncillo*, water, rum, star anise, *canela*, clove, and anise seeds in a pot. There should be just enough liquid to cover the sugar. Bring to boil, reduce to a simmer, and cook until the liquid reduces to a syrup consistency, 7 or 8 minutes (see headnote), and set aside. Let the spices steep in the liquid as it cools completely at room temperature, about 1 hour, then strain.

MACADAMIA-CHIPOTLE BRITTLE

1 ½ cups sugar

¾ cup light Karo syrup

½ cup water

1 ½ tablespoons unsalted butter

½ tablespoon ground *chipotle* powder

⅛ teaspoon baking soda

½ pound macadamia nuts, coarsely chopped and lightly toasted

TO ASSEMBLE SUNDAE:

1. For each sundae, pour 1 tablespoon of *Piloncillo*-Rum Syrup in the bottom of a sundae dish. Add 1 teaspoon of Macadamia-*Chipotle* Brittle and 1 scoop of Coconut Ice Cream; layer with another tablespoon of syrup and brittle.

2. Add a scoop of Tamarind Sorbet, and layer with another tablespoon of syrup and brittle. Add another scoop of coconut ice cream, another tablespoon of syrup and brittle, and finally top with whipped cream and a sprinkle of crushed brittle.

1. Lightly butter a jellyroll pan.

2. In a medium saucepan, combine the sugar, corn syrup, and water and stir over medium-low heat until the sugar dissolves. Increase the heat to medium and, using a wooden spoon, stir slowly but constantly until the mixture reaches a light golden color, about 20 minutes.

3. Immediately remove from heat, add the butter, *chipotle* powder, and baking soda and stir until very foamy. Quickly stir in the macadamia nuts and pour at once onto the prepared pan. Cool completely and coarsely chop the brittle.

THROUGHOUT MEXICO AND LATIN AMERICA, SOUR-TASTING TAMARIND IS USED AS A FOIL FOR SUGAR IN SAVORY AND SWEET DISHES. IT'S ALSO COOKED WITH SUGAR AND DIPPED IN CHILE POWDER AS CANDY.

OAXACAN SQUASH TEA
AGUA DE CHILACAYOTA /// 237

HIBISCUS TEA
AGUA DE JAMAICA /// 239

MINTED HONEYDEW AGUA FRESCA
AGUA DE MELÓN VERDE /// 239

BLACKBERRY LEMONADE
LIMONADA DE MORAS /// 240

PRICKLY PEAR AND CELERY AGUA FRESCA
AGUA DE FRUTAS DE TUNAS Y APIO /// 241

COCONUT HORCHATA
HORCHATA DE COCO /// 243

SPICED COFFEE
CAFÉ DE OLLA /// 244

MEXICAN HOT CHOCOLATE
TAZA DE CHOCOLATE /// 245

BEER AND CLAM-TOMATO JUICE COCKTAIL
CHELATO /// 248

PINEAPPLE BEER
TEPACHE /// 250

GREEN BLOODY MARY
BLOODY MARY VERDE /// 253

Aguas Frescas

In Mexico, there is a whole group of refreshing cold drinks called *aguas frescas*. Typically they are made with water, fruit, and a sweetener, but there are others made with dried flowers and even squashes or seeds. Street vendors commonly serve them from a barrel-shaped clear jar called a *vitrolero*.

These thirst-quenchers aren't meant to be overly sweet. To ensure that the sweetener—white sugar, *piloncillo* (brown sugar), or agave nectar—is fully dissolved, some fruits, like berries, can be macerated with the sugar. In others, the sugar is cooked with the ingredients or sugar syrup is added. The key is to highlight the flavor of the main ingredients.

OAXACAN SQUASH TEA
AGUA DE CHILACAYOTA

Yield: Serves 6 (3 quarts)

This unusual but surprisingly delicious agua fresca is typically found in Oaxaca. I urge you to try it. It is made with chilacayota squash, which is similar to our spaghetti squash. But you can use any winter squash, including a pumpkin. Traditionally locals add a scoop of cooling sorbet, such as lime, before serving it. Our Pineapple-Lime Sorbet (page 228) is even tastier.

Pineapple-Lime Sorbet (page 228, optional)

1 (3-pound) chilacayota squash, split in half, seeds removed, and cut into medium-size cubes

2 quarts water

2 (6-ounce) cones *piloncillo*

2 (4-inch) sticks *canela* (Mexican cinnamon)

1 pineapple, peeled and diced

Grated zest of 1 lime

1. Prepare the Pineapple-Lime Sorbet, if using.

2. In a large saucepan, combine the squash, water, *piloncillo*, and *canela*; simmer over medium-low heat until the squash is soft and the pulp can be removed easily. With a slotted spoon, remove the squash from the pan and discard the rind.

3. Return the flesh to the pan along with the liquid and mash with a handheld blender until almost smooth. Scrape into a bowl and cool to room temperature; refrigerate until very cold, about 2 hours.

4. Add the pineapple and lime zest and stir until combined. Serve in tall glasses over ice with a scoop of Pineapple-Lime Sorbet, if desired.

HIBISCUS TEA

AGUA DE JAMAICA

Yield: Serves 4

6 cups water

2 cups (2 ounces) dried *jamaica* flowers (hibiscus)

¾ cup sugar

1 (3-inch) piece fresh ginger, cut into ½-inch slices

I vividly remember the first time I tasted this refreshing drink made with dried hibiscus flowers. My family and I were in Mexico (I was probably about eight) and the dazzling color was entrancing. Later I discovered the drink is ubiquitous in taquerías throughout the country. It has the added benefit of being high in vitamin C.

1. In a medium saucepan, bring the water to a boil. Add the flowers, sugar, and ginger and boil for 1 minute, stirring continuously. Pour into a nonreactive bowl and steep for 2 hours.

2. Pour the mixture through a strainer into a bowl, pressing on the flower solids and ginger to extract as much liquid as possible. Taste for strength and sweetness. If it is too potent, add water or, if too tart, add more sugar. Cover and refrigerate until ready to serve.

MINTED HONEYDEW AGUA FRESCA

AGUA DE MELÓN VERDE

Yield: Serves 4

2 cups water

⅓ to ½ cup sugar

4 cups cubed honeydew melon

5 or 6 large fresh mint leaves

1 tablespoon freshly squeezed lime juice

A hint of fresh mint really bumps up the flavor in this pale green agua fresca. Everyone at Dos Caminos seems to think that a splash of something—like silver tequila or white rum—makes it taste better . . . and I totally agree.

Combine the water and sugar in a small saucepan and bring to a simmer, stirring to dissolve the sugar. In the jar of an electric blender, combine the syrup with the honeydew, mint leaves, and lime juice and blend at high speed until smooth, working in batches if necessary. Chill and serve in tall glasses over crushed or cubed ice.

BLACKBERRY LEMONADE

LIMONADA DE MORAS

Yield: Serves 4 to 6

6 lemons, scrubbed
2 cups water, divided
1 cup sugar
½ cup fresh blackberries
2 cups ice cubes
Lemon slices, for garnish

Beautiful deep purple blackberries are readily available in Mexico, so it's easy to find this refreshing lemonade. It's a real treat.

1. With a vegetable peeler or paring knife, remove the zest from 4 lemons and squeeze enough juice from these and the remaining 2 lemons to measure 1 cup.

2. In a saucepan, combine 1 cup of the water with the sugar and bring to a boil; cook until the sugar dissolves, stirring often. Add the zest, lemon juice, and remaining 1 cup of water. Remove from the heat and let the mixture cool.

3. In the jar of an electric blender, purée the blackberries and stir into the lemonade. Pour the blackberry lemonade through a fine strainer into a pitcher, cover, and chill until very cold. Serve the lemonade over ice in tall glasses garnished with lemon slices.

PRICKLY PEAR AND CELERY AGUA FRESCA

AGUA DE FRUTAS DE TUNAS Y APIO

Yield: Serves 2

4 prickly pears, peeled (see sidebar)

2 medium stalks celery

¼ cup sugar

Juice of 2 limes, plus slices for garnish

¼ teaspoon ground cinnamon, preferably *canela* (Mexican cinnamon)

2 cups crushed ice

Prickly pears have a spectacular, otherworldly magenta color that is almost unnatural. Here the fruit is blended with celery into a tasty, refreshing aqua fresca. By the way, no one is really sure why prickly pears are called "tunas" in Spanish. One of the myths is that it is because they resemble the color of the fish's flesh, and the shape is similar, as well.

In the jar of an electric blender, purée the pears and celery; pass the liquid through a fine strainer. Combine the liquid, sugar, lime juice, cinnamon, and ice in the blender and purée for 1 minute. Pour into tall glasses with ice, garnish with lime slices, and serve.

PRICKLY PEAR FRUIT (*TUNAS*) AND HOW TO PEEL THEM

IN MEXICO, THE FRUITS OF THE PRICKLY PEAR CACTUS ARE CALLED *TUNAS*. THEY HAVE NUMEROUS TINY SPINES THAT MUST BE CAREFULLY PEELED BEFORE EATING. THE FRUIT IS SERVED CHILLED OR AT ROOM TEMPERATURE. IT IS ALSO USED AS THE BASE FOR PRICKLY PEAR JAMS AND JELLIES, AS WELL AS MEXICAN CACTUS CANDY AND A REFRESHING AGUA FRESCA.

COCONUT HORCHATA
HORCHATA DE COCO

Yield: Serves 4

2 ⅔ cups (19 ounces) uncooked rice, finely ground in a spice grinder

1 teaspoon crumbled *canela* (Mexican cinnamon), plus 4 (4-inch) pieces for garnish

4 cups hot water, plus 1 cup cold water

15 blanched almonds, lightly toasted and finely ground

1 (13 ½-ounce) can coconut milk

1 cup sugar

1 cup cold water

Zest of 1 lime, cut into long, ½-inch-wide strips

Ice cubes

4 ounces light rum (optional)

6 to 8 fresh mint sprigs, for garnish

This version is from Veracruz, one of Mexico's hottest regions, and is served both in restaurants and by street vendors, like an agua fresca. While not difficult to make, it is made in two parts, the first a day ahead. Although pure white, horchata isn't made with cow's milk, so it's ideal for anyone with dairy allergies.

1. One day in advance, combine the rice, *canela*, and 4 cups of hot water in a bowl. Cool, cover, and refrigerate.

2. The following day, stir the ground almonds and coconut milk into the rice. Working in batches, add the rice mixture to the jar of an electric blender and process until very smooth. Strain through a medium-size strainer and pour into a pitcher.

3. In a saucepan over low heat, combine the sugar, the remaining cup of cold water, and lime zest. Cook until the sugar is just dissolved, stirring continuously. Let the mixture cool, remove the lime zest, pour the liquid into the pitcher, and mix well. Cover and refrigerate until chilled.

4. Stir well and pour over ice cubes into tall glasses. If desired, add an ounce of rum to each glass before adding the horchata. Garnish with a mint sprig and a piece of cinnamon.

HORCHATA IS AN EXTREMELY REFRESHING COOL DRINK MADE WITH RICE LIQUID SWEETENED WITH SUGAR AND FLAVORED WITH CINNAMON AND LIME. IT IS THOUGHT TO HAVE ORIGINATED IN EGYPT AND LATER TO HAVE BEEN CARRIED TO THE IBERIAN PENINSULA. WHEN SPANIARDS CAME TO MEXICO, THEIR VERSION OF THE DRINK WAS MADE WITH CHUFA NUTS. LOCALS QUICKLY SUBSTITUTED RICE.

SPICED COFFEE
CAFÉ DE OLLA

Yield: Serves 4 (6-ounce cups)

Mexico grows a lot of coffee and it's delicious. The standard beverage for breakfast is freshly brewed coffee scented with spices. (The other choice is Mexican Hot Chocolate, page 245.) Very early in the morning, around market squares, the air is pungent with this robust aroma. The comedors who sell coffee from carts use a whisk-like tool called a molinillo to froth hot milk (see sidebar). It was brought by Spaniards when they conquered Mexico in the sixteenth century.

4 cups water

6 ounces *piloncillo* (1 cone) or 1 cup firmly packed dark brown sugar plus 2 teaspoons molasses added to it

2 (4-inch) sticks *canela* (Mexican cinnamon)

½ teaspoon anise seeds

1 cup (3 ounces) medium roast coffee, medium to coarse grind

2 cups low-fat milk

1. In a medium saucepan, combine the water with the *piloncillo*, *canela*, and anise seeds. Slowly bring the liquid to a boil over medium heat, stirring to melt the sugar. Stir in the coffee, remove from the heat, cover, and steep for 5 minutes.

2. In a small saucepan, heat the milk over medium-high heat and whisk until it is frothy. Or heat the milk in the microwave. Strain the coffee through a fine strainer into cups and serve immediately. Serve with the frothed milk on the side.

 ## MOLINILLO DE MADERA

MEXICANS USE THIS HANDY TURNED WOODEN TOOL TO FOAM MILK. IT WAS ORIGINALLY MADE BY EIGHTEENTH-CENTURY SPANISH SETTLERS TO MEXICO TO FROTH HOT CHOCOLATE. EARLY VERSIONS FIT INSIDE A TALL CONTAINER AND THE USER THEN ROTATED THE TOOL BETWEEN HIS TWO HANDS, PALMS TOGETHER, TO MAKE THE LIQUID FOAMY. MEXICANS DON'T GENERALLY SERVE CAPPUCCINO BUT LOVE COFFEE WITH STEAMED MILK. A MOLINILLO MAKES THE LOCAL VERSION OF CAPPUCCINO EASY. YOU CAN FIND THE TOOL ON MEXGROCER.COM.

MEXICAN HOT CHOCOLATE
TAZA DE CHOCOLATE

Yield: Serves 4

If good coffee is a passion in Mexico, chocolate is an obsession. If you don't have coffee in the morning, you will certainly have hot chocolate. For breakfast, Mexican hot chocolate is made with the local grainy chocolate that is flavored with sugar, cinnamon, and almonds and blended with hot whole milk.

This is my fancy version of the drink, and I think it's also a sophisticated way to finish dinner, especially if you stir a couple tablespoons of brandy into the cup.

2 cups whole milk

¼ teaspoon ground cinnamon, preferably *canela* (Mexican cinnamon)

1 stick *canela* (Mexican cinnamon), plus 4 (4-inch) sticks, for garnish

1 (2-inch) strip orange zest

1 ounce semisweet chocolate, chopped into small pieces

⅛ teaspoon pure vanilla extract

Whipped cream, for garnish

In a heavy saucepan, heat the milk, ground cinnamon, 1 *canela* stick, and orange zest over medium heat until simmering. Add the chocolate and let it melt, stirring occasionally. Remove from the heat, remove the orange zest, and stir in the vanilla. Ladle the chocolate into mugs and serve garnished with a generous dollop of whipped cream and a *canela* stick.

Chocolate: A Love Affair

I think there is simply no better start to the day than laying a piece of rich dark chocolate dipped in coffee on my tongue and letting its luscious taste dissolve. Many Mexicans are similarly fanatic about chocolate for breakfast, except they typically enjoy theirs as a cup of hot chocolate (page 245) . . . and I continue to eat mine all day. It's a passion.

Mexicans have been obsessed with chocolate since the Mayan people began cultivating the evergreen *Theobroma cacao L.* trees in the Yucatán rainforest. Almost two thousand years ago, this early culture had remarkably figured out the process of opening the cacao pods, fermenting and drying the beans, and then roasting and grinding them into a paste as a base for a beverage.

The Aztecs subsequently acquired cacao through trade with the Mayans, and by the fifteenth century, they had elevated it to a food for royalty, high-ranking military officers, and religious rituals. The name *Theobroma* means "food of the gods."

When the Spanish explorer Hernán Cortés and his men came to Tenochtitlán to meet with Montezuma in 1519, the Aztec emperor was drinking xocóatl, or "bitter water," made with ground cacao beans, vanilla, and spices boiled in water. His court reputedly drank about two thousand cups of the beverage a day—fifty by the emperor himself, according to an exhibit about chocolate at Chicago's Field Museum.

The unsweetened beverage (sugar only reached the New World with Columbus) was served in golden vessels and the Spaniards were dazzled by the drink's seemingly mind-altering properties. After Cortés conquered the Aztecs in 1521, he returned to Spain with chocolate as one of the culinary treasures on board his ships.

Spanish aristocrats took to the drink immediately but preferred their newly acquired, secret beverage sweetened, so sugar was added when the liquid was heated. But secrets have a way of escaping, and ultimately, clerics leaked chocolate across the border to the French court; within hundred years it had been introduced to London and Switzerland and the world. Today, as with those early traders, the product is still considered an elixir or magic potion by many.

Over time, as luxury chocolates became smoother, Mexican chocolate retained its character: rustic and grainy in texture from the sugar granules and cacao bits that remain after it is ground on natural millstones. It is not especially sweet. Today Mexican chocolate is still typically flavored with ground almonds, vanilla, cinnamon, and sometimes chile pepper; it is sold in 3-ounce disks. Abuelita and Ibarra are the most readily available brands online and in ethnic markets.

Besides hot chocolate for breakfast, the other dish in which Mexican chocolate has pride of place is in the *mole* sauces of Oaxaca and Puebla. These celebrated sauces aren't sweet but the small amount of chocolate added to them imparts a complexity to the flavor that, once you taste it, is definitely missed when absent.

Oaxaca is "Chocolate Central," where they live and breathe the stuff. I've been there six times. But last year I had a pivotal chocolate moment in Tepoztlán, about ninety minutes south of Mexico City, where I roasted my own beans, took them to the molino, or mill, to have them ground, and then pressed the chocolate into molds by hand. The smell and taste were the deepest, richest, and most chocolately I'd ever experienced.

Until recently, the chocolate we used at Dos Caminos was made for us in Oaxaca and imported. Not long ago, we discovered Taza, a wonderful free-trade chocolate company in Massachusetts with its own molino. Their organic chocolates are stone-ground on an old Oaxacan mill and minimally processed, so now we have real Mexican chocolate made in the United States.

From a kid growing up on Reese's Peanut Butter Cups and M&Ms, to an adult with training and a lot of tasting, I've come to appreciate chocolate more fully. Along the way I discovered Valrhona and Maison du Chocolate, but I also live up the street from Jacques Torres, who does chocolate-covered Cheerios and an ice-cream version of his Wicked Hot Chocolate, and I stop by most summer Sundays for a scoop: Wicked for me, vanilla for Frida and Diego, my dachshunds!

What I love about Mexican chocolate is that it was discovered there and has been a staple of the culture for millennia. It's still drunk as a beverage and passed on as a tradition, and it continues to play an important role to this day. This amazing indigenous ingredient adds a depth of flavor that hasn't been used in other cuisines, and in which you can still taste the earth.

BEER AND CLAM-TOMATO JUICE COCKTAIL

CHELATO

Yield: Serves 1

¼ cup Clamato juice cocktail

1 (12-ounce) can or bottle Mexican beer

Dash *each* of salt, black pepper, celery salt, Maggi sauce, and Valentina hot sauce

Splash Rose's lime juice

2 wedges key lime

This zesty combination of beer, clam-tomato juice, and spices is a must with Tacos Campechanos (page 121), like those found at Taquería Villamelon at the bullring in the Distrito Federal in Mexico City.

Fill a 16-ounce glass with ice. Pour the Clamato juice over the ice and add the beer. Stir in the salt, pepper, celery salt, Maggi and Valentina sauces, and Rose's lime juice. Squeeze one lime wedge over the drink and garnish the glass with the other lime wedge. Enjoy!

PINEAPPLE BEER

TEPACHE

Yield: Serves 8

This fizzy drink made with fermented pineapple is enjoyed throughout Mexico's Central West Coast, as well as in Mexico City.

1 large ripe golden pineapple, crown and base removed, outside scrubbed and rinsed

2 whole allspice berries

2 whole cloves

1 (4-inch) stick *canela* (Mexican cinnamon)

10 ½ cups water, divided

1 pound *piloncillo*, crushed or 1 pound firmly-packed dark brown sugar

1 ½ cups light beer

TRADITIONALLY, LEFTOVER PEELINGS AND CORES WERE USED TO MAKE THE BEVERAGE AND FERMENTATION TOOK MANY DAYS. WE AT DOS CAMINOS, AND MANY MODERN MEXICANS, USE THE WHOLE FRUIT AND ADD BEER TO SPEED UP THE PROCESS.

---

1. Cut the unpeeled pineapple into 1 ½-inch cubes. Combine the allspice, cloves, and *canela* in a mortar and crush roughly with a pestle. Transfer to a 4- to 5-quart earthenware or glass jar with a tight-fitting lid.

2. Add the pineapple cubes and 8 cups of the water and stir to combine. Cover the jar with a lid and set it in a location that receives plenty of sun (or in a warm spot) until the mixture begins to ferment and bubbles form on the top, about 3 days.

3. In a small saucepan, combine the *piloncillo* and remaining 2 ½ cups of water and bring to a boil over medium-high heat; reduce the heat to medium-low and simmer, stirring occasionally, until the sugar has completely dissolved, 4 to 5 minutes.

4. Remove the pan from the heat, let the syrup cool slightly, and then add it along with the beer to the fermenting pineapple mixture. Stir well, cover, and leave in a warm place for 2 to 3 days longer, or until it smells strongly fermented and appears bubbly throughout.

5. Strain the mixture through a fine-mesh strainer lined with a few layers of cheesecloth into a clean jar; discard the cheesecloth and refrigerate the liquid until cold. Serve over ice. (This is especially good with a Veracruz cigar!)

GREEN BLOODY MARY

BLOODY MARY VERDE

Yield: Serves 6

This is my updated version of the iconic brunch drink.

6 ounces homemade or purchased Chile Vodka (recipe follows)

2 ½ pounds ripe tomatillos, husked and chopped

1 pound cucumbers, peeled, seeded, and diced

¼ cup packed, torn fresh basil leaves

1 *serrano* chile, seeds and membranes removed, if desired, chopped

1 teaspoon Worcestershire sauce

1 teaspoon Valentina sauce

½ teaspoon sea salt

¼ teaspoon freshly ground black pepper

Finely chopped small celery leaves, plus 6 small whole leaves, for garnish

1. Make the Chile Vodka (below) or buy it.

2. Combine the tomatillos, cucumbers, basil leaves, *serrano* chile, Worcestershire and Valentina sauces, salt, and pepper in a food processor and purée until smooth. Divide the liquid among 6 tall glasses filled with crushed ice. Pour 1 ounce of Chile Vodka in each glass. Sprinkle with chopped celery leaves and garnish with 1 whole celery leaf.

TO MAKE CHILE VODKA

1 (750ml) bottle vodka

10 *serrano* or *jalapeño* peppers (or to taste), cut in half

Combine the vodka and chile peppers in a bottle and put it in the freezer for at least 2 days before using.

CLASSIC MARGARITA
MARGARITA CLASSICO

Yield: Serves 2

1 ounce Simple Syrup (recipe follows)

1 tablespoon Lime-Salt-Sugar (recipe follows)

3 ounces 100 percent agave silver tequila

2 ounces freshly squeezed lime juice

½ to 1 teaspoon orange liqueur

Lime wedges, to garnish

SIMPLE SYRUP

Yield: 1 ½ cups

1 cup sugar

1 cup water

Combine the sugar and water in a small saucepan and cook over low heat, stirring, until the sugar dissolves. Remove and cool. You can store extra syrup in a sealed container in the refrigerator for up to 1 month.

Who doesn't love a perfect margarita? Here are the basics to make the real drink, not the "tarted up" versions you find in many watering holes. Use any leftover Simple Syrup to sweeten iced tea or agua fresca. There is absolutely no substitute for freshly squeezed lime juice in a margarita.

1. Make the Simple Syrup and Lime-Salt-Sugar (below).

2. Fill a cocktail shaker with ice. Add the tequila, lime juice, Simple Syrup, and orange liqueur. Cover and shake until mixed and chilled, about 30 seconds.

3. Pour the Lime-Salt-Sugar onto a plate. Press the rims of 2 chilled rocks or wine glasses into the mixture to rim the edge. Strain the margarita into the glasses and serve.

LIME-SALT-SUGAR

Yield: ¼ cup

Zest of 1 lime

2 tablespoons kosher salt

2 tablespoons sugar

Combine the lime, salt, and sugar in a small blender or mini food chopper and blend until finely chopped.

PASSION FRUIT MARGARITA

MARGARITA DE FRUTA PASIÓN

Yield: Serves 8

3 cups passion fruit juice

Juice of 4 limes

2 ½ cups *reposado* tequila

½ cup Grand Marnier

Raspberries, for garnish

Combine all of the ingredients except the raspberries in a bowl and stir well. Refrigerate until ready to use. Pour into a cocktail shaker with ice and shake vigorously to combine. Strain into margarita glasses over ice and garnish with raspberries.

HIBISCUS MARGARITA

MARGARITA DE JAMAICA

Yield: Serves 1

3 ounces chilled Agua de Jamaica (page 239)

1 ½ ounces 100 percent agave silver tequila

1 ounce Simple Syrup (page 254)

Juice of 1 lime

Lime wedge, for garnish

Pour the Agua de Jamaica, tequila, simple syrup, and lime juice into a chilled cocktail shaker filled with ice. Shake well. Strain into a chilled margarita glass and garnish with a lime wedge.

AVOCADO MARGARITA
MARGARITA DE AGUACATE

Yield: Serves 4

The color and flavor of this creamy, fruity margarita are so beautiful, it doesn't need any garnish.

Coarse salt, to rim the glasses

2 cups crushed ice

¾ cup 100 percent agave silver tequila

½ cup freshly squeezed lime juice

¼ cup triple sec

1 avocado, preferably Hass variety, peeled, pitted, and diced

1 sprig fresh cilantro

Rim 4 margarita glasses with salt. Combine the ice, tequila, lime juice, triple sec, avocado, and cilantro in the jar of an electric blender and blend until smooth. Pour into the glasses and serve.

MOM'S MARGARITA
MARGARITA DE MAMI

Yield: Serves 1

2 tablespoons freshly squeezed lime juice

1 ounce 100 percent agave silver tequila

1 ounce Cointreau or triple sec

1 teaspoon orange flower water

3 ounces champagne

1 slice lime, to garnish

We serve this special margarita on Mother's Day at Dos Caminos. It's made with a combination of champagne and orange flower water.

Combine the lime juice, tequila, triple sec, and orange flower water in a shaker filled with ice. Shake vigorously until very cold and strain into a champagne flute. Slash with champagne and garnish with a lime slice.

WATERMELON-CUCUMBER MARGARITA

MARGARITA DE SANDÍA Y PEPINO

Yield: Serves 2

1 ½ cups roughly chopped watermelon

6 (⅛-inch-thick) slices seedless cucumber

10 large fresh mint leaves

½ cup 100 percent agave silver tequila

¼ cup freshly squeezed lime juice

2 tablespoons Simple Syrup (page 254)

1 tablespoon orange liqueur

2 cups ice cubes

2 small watermelon triangles, each skewered on a bar pick with 1 cucumber round, to garnish

2 fresh mint sprigs, to garnish

1. Combine the watermelon, cucumber, and mint leaves in a food mill or in a colander and set over a medium bowl. Process the mixture through the food mill or press firmly on the solids with a muddler or wooden spoon until mashed.

2. Pour the fruit juice into a shaker. Add the tequila, lime juice, Simple Syrup, and orange liqueur, and 1 cup of ice. Top with the shaker glass and shake to blend well. Strain into 2 tall glasses filled with ice and garnish with watermelon skewers and mint sprigs.

BLACK BULL

TORO NEGRO

Yield: Serves 1

This little cantina drink is simply tequila with a bottle of Mexican cola. I added Lemon Salt to be fancy and it bumps up the flavor. It'd be perfect for el Día de los Muertos (Halloween). As a bar snack, the Spiced Peanuts (page 261) are great.

2 ounces 100 percent agave silver tequila

1 bottle Mexican cola

Lemon Salt (recipe follows)

Lemon wedges

1. Make the Lemon Salt (below).

2. Rub the rim of a highball glass with a lemon. Dip the rim into the Lemon Salt and fill with ice.

3. Add the tequila and fill the glass half full with cola. Squeeze a quarter of a lime into the glass and then garnish with a wedge of lemon. Serve the remaining cola on the side.

LEMON SALT

1 cup kosher salt

2 tablespoons sugar

Zest of 4 lemons

Combine the salt, sugar, and lemon zests in a spice grinder, food processor, or blender and process until finely ground. Store in an airtight container.

SPICED PEANUTS
CACAHUATES GARAPINADOS

Yield: 2 cups

These wonderful nibbles are amazing paired with a margarita or Toro Negro.

2 cups shelled unsalted peanuts with the skin on

2 tablespoons unsalted butter

¼ cup firmly packed light brown sugar

½ teaspoon *chipotle* powder

½ teaspoon freshly ground *canela* (Mexican cinnamon stick)

½ teaspoon salt

1. Line a cookie sheet with parchment paper.

2. Toast the peanuts in a dry skillet over medium heat, stirring frequently, until they begin to brown around the edges, about 4 minutes; remove from the pan and set aside.

3. Return the hot pan to the heat and add the butter. When the butter melts, stir in the sugar, *chipotle* powder, cinnamon, and salt and cook until the sugar has melted. Add the peanuts and continue stirring for about 2 more minutes or until the peanuts are glazed and golden brown.

4. Transfer the peanuts to the cookie sheet and separate them with a fork. Let them cool until the glaze has hardened; store in an airtight container.

TEQUILA PUNCH
PONCHE
Yield: Serves at least 16

I adore sangria, but if you order that drink in Mexico, you get red wine mixed with lemonade. This combination is a sparkly option for a fiesta.

8 cups diced fresh fruits, such as melon, pineapple, apples, pears, and halved grapes

4 cups chilled silver tequila

3 cups chilled dry champagne

3 cups chilled Sauternes

½ cup Simple Syrup (page 254) or to taste

Juice of 1 lime

In a large punch bowl, combine all ingredients and stir over ice cubes.

SANGRITA
Yield: Serves 12 or more

This is my friend Scott's take on a spicy Mexican drink that means "little blood," traditionally made with the juice of tomatoes, oranges, limes, and chiles. Don't confuse it with sangria, the fruity drink. This definitely has a kick and is served as a chaser for tequila.

2 cups tomato juice

1 cup orange juice

¾ cup grapefruit juice

½ cup freshly squeezed lime juice

2 tablespoons pomegranate molasses

1 tablespoon Maggi sauce

1 tablespoon Worcestershire sauce

1 tablespoon Valentina hot sauce

1 tablespoon Tabasco sauce

1 tablespoons kosher salt

1 bottle premium tequila, served as shots on the side

In a very large container, mix all the ingredients except the tequila and chill. Serve straight up with a shot of tequila.

ACKNOWLEDGMENTS

Dos Caminos Mexican Street Food was created with friendship, love, and help from my family, friends, and colleagues. My mother Charlene, father Russ, and sister Holly were as always proud, enthusiastic, and supportive. I could not have done it without them and the constant adoring affection of my dachshunds Frida and Diego—the best stress medicine ever.

My utmost gratitude goes to Stephen Hanson, founder and president of BR Guest Hospitality, who allowed me the opportunity to write this book, and to Donna Rodriguez, our vice president of marketing, for putting all of the pieces together and making it happen.

Included in the large group of colleagues was Brian Mannett, my meticulous recipe tester and Dos Caminos executive chef; Sarah Shapiro, my chief assistant food stylist and Dos Caminos executive chef; and "all-around help me with anything I needed ASAP" person, Meghan Young, Dos Caminos executive chef. Hugo Reyes, our pastry chef, contributed both ideas and recipe testing. A special thanks to my best friend and co-corporate chef at Dos Caminos, Scott Linquist. Our collaboration on the food at Dos Caminos has been one of the most rewarding aspects of my career.

To the staff in all of the kitchens and dining rooms of Dos Caminos, I am forever grateful for your professionalism and friendship that motivate me every day. I am also grateful to all the support staff at BR Guest Hospitality, as well as all my fellow chefs and managers, who have shared their ideas, camaraderie, and advice throughout the years.

Additional thanks to current and past mentors: Chris Giarraputo, Brett Reichler, Normand Laprise, Andy D'Amico, Gary Robins, Mary Sue Milliken, and Susan Feniger.

As well as writing about food, I love to read about it and have been inspired creatively by these books and find myself constantly consulting them, and so they deserve credit too: *The Essential Cuisines of*

Mexico, Diana Kennedy; *On Food and Cooking*, Harold McGee; *Culinary Artistry*, Andrew Dornenburg and Karen Page; *Food from My Heart*, Zarela Martinez; *Spice*, Ana Sortun; *American Cookery*, James Beard; and of course, the book that started it all, *Mastering the Art of French Cooking*, Simone Beck, Louisette Bertholle, and Julia Child.

Thanks to Alan "Battman" Batt for the beautiful photographs and Ann Treistman, our editor at Skyhorse Publishing, for believing in my idea.

And, of course, a final thanks to my collaborator Joanna Pruess. I am not a writer by any means but a chef who is passionate about Mexican food and loves to share it with food lovers. This book would not have been possible without Joanna by my side to help me translate my thoughts to paper. Thank you for everything.

Ivy Stark

APPENDIX A
CHILE GLOSSARY
GLOSARIO DE CHILES

Chiles or chile peppers are the fruit of plants from the genus *Capsicum*, which are members of the nightshade family *Solanaceae*. Even though they may be thought of as a vegetable, their culinary usage is generally as a spice. The part of the plant that is usually harvested is the fruit, and botany considers the plant itself a berry shrub. San Diego, California, and the Florida peninsula may be the only locales in the United States where tropical perennials such as chile peppers frequently survive from one growing season to the next.

The name, which is spelled differently in many regions (chili, chile, or chilli) comes from Nahuatl via the Spanish word *chile*. The term "chile" in most of the world refers exclusively to the smaller hot types of *capsicum*. The large mild types are called "bell peppers" in the United States; simply "pepper" in Britain, Canada, and Ireland; "capsicum" in India and Australia; and "paprika" in many European countries.

Although chile peppers and their various cultivars originated in the Americas, they are now grown around the world because they are widely used as spices or vegetables in many cuisines and also prized for their medicinal value.

While even the same variety of chiles can vary in the intensity of heat—some *jalapeños* are quite mild while others are pretty intense—a general rule to help determine the heat of chile peppers is: the smaller the top, where it's attached to the stem, the hotter it is.

That said, some chiles ripen from green to red, and become milder and sweeter in taste. Also, the hottest parts of a chile are the membranes inside next to the seeds. If you want a somewhat milder flavor, remove them before using. Finally, when handling chile peppers, always wear gloves and never touch your eyes or nose.

Chile Glossary

Dried

Chile Ancho: A *poblano* pepper that has been ripened and dried, it is triangular in shape with broad shoulders tapering to a blunt tip. Deep red in color with a wrinkled, shiny skin, *anchos* average 4 ½ inches

long and 3 inches across the top. Most are mild with a fruity, slightly acid flavor, but some may be hot, depending on where they were grown, the soil, the amount of water received during the growing season, and the climate of the land. Similar in size and shape to the *mulato* pepper, *anchos* can be distinguished by holding them up to a light: an *ancho* will have a reddish hue and the *mulato* will be chocolate brown.

Chile de Árbol: Ripened to bright red and dried, *chile de árbol* comes from a short plant, rather than a tree as the name implies. It is a smooth-skinned, slender chile that tapers to a sharp point and generally measures about 3 inches long and ⅜ inch wide. Thin fleshed and very, very hot, these chiles develop a sharp flavor when lightly toasted. They are mostly used for hot table sauces, for frying whole and adding to dishes, like a pot of beans, or ground to a powder for a condiment for sliced fruit, cucumbers, or jicama.

Chile Cascabel: a deep reddish sphere with a smooth polished surface, it rattles when shaken, as the name implies. Available throughout Mexico, chile *cascabel* is predominantly used for table sauces, but also incorporated into the dishes of the central-western and the northern parts of the country. Pleasantly hot and measuring on average about 1 ¼ inches wide and 1 inch long, *cascabels* become quite fleshy when rehydrated.

Chile Chipotle: A ripened, smoke-dried *jalapeño*, the name derives from the Nahuatl words for chile (*chil*) and smoke (*pectli*). There are two varieties of the *chipotle* pepper: *chipotle mora*, which is mulberry colored, and the larger *meco*, which is tobacco brown (it is grown red and dries to that color). The average *chipotle* is 2 ½ inches long and about 1 inch wide, very spicy, and becomes quite fleshy when rehydrated. The versatile *chipotle* is used for pickling, as well as for flavoring soups, sauces, fish, and meat dishes. They are also available canned, packed in adobo.

Chile Costeño: As the name implies, it is grown in Northern Oaxaca and Costal Guerrero, as well as the Mixteca Baja, where it is used almost exclusively. Averaging about 3 ½ inches in length and about ½ inch wide, tapering to a pointed tip, the *chile costeño* is a beautiful bronzy-red color with a thin, almost transparent, shiny skin. Most often they are dried, but sometimes they may be sold when ripe, but still green. Costeños range in sharpness from very hot to pleasantly mild. There is also a less popular bronzy-yellow variety from the same area, which is usually used toasted and ground with garlic, salt, and water for a rustic table sauce, sometimes with tomatoes added. They are also used in the local *moles* and sauces for flavoring tamales.

Chile Guajillo: Literally meaning "big pod," this is the chile, along with the *ancho*, most commonly used in Mexico. Inexpensive and readily available, it is reddish in color with a tough, opaque, shiny, smooth skin and shaped like an elongated triangle with narrow

shoulders tapering to a pointed tip. An average-size *guajillo* measures 1 ¼ inches across the top and about 5 inches long, and has a crisp, sharp flavor that can vary from very hot to fairly hot. When rehydrated, *guajillos* are fleshy on the inside, but their skin remains tough, so sauces made with them are usually strained. *Guajillos* are versatile and used for table sauces, enchiladas, adobos (seasoning pastes), and stews.

Chile Mulato: gets its name from its brown color. The plant is essentially the same as the *poblano* with slightly different genes that affect the color and the taste of the fruit. When mature, these chiles are a very dark green but then deepen to a rich brown as they ripen. *Mulatos* range from mild to fairly hot and have a sweetish taste that, along with their color, makes them perfectly suitable for *mole poblano.* When rehydrated, they are fleshy and have a mild, faint chocolate taste.

Chile Pasilla: The dried form of the *chile chilaca,* its name simply means large. Also known as *chile negro* in some parts of Mexico, *pasillas* are long and narrow with blunt or slightly pointed ends and shiny black, puckered skin displaying vertical ridges. An average-size *chile pasilla* is about 6 inches long and 1 inch wide. In flavor, *pasillas* range from hot to fairly hot, and when rehydrated, they have a sharp but rich flavor. Also very versatile, *pasillas* can be used in table sauces and *moles,* or stuffed, fried whole, or cut into strips for a garnish. The toasted veins are also used as a condiment.

Chile Pasilla de Oaxaca: A unique and delicious chile used almost exclusively in Oaxaca and in a limited part of neighboring Puebla, it is grown in small quantities in very isolated valleys in extremely rugged terrain. Usually left to ripen on the plant and then smoked in rustic conditions, they tend to be fruity and smoky, but also extremely hot. Like the *pasilla,* it has a shiny, wrinkled skin and pointed tip, varies in length, and is fleshy when rehydrated. This rare chile is expensive, and usually sold by count of 100 rather than by weight.

Fresh

Habanero Chile: An extremely hot chile pepper, it is native to the Caribbean, the Yucatán, and the north coast of South America. Small and lantern-shaped, the habanero ranges from light green to bright orange when ripe. It's generally used for sauces in both its fresh and dried form.

Jalapeño Chile: Named after Jalapa, the capital of Veracruz, Mexico, this smooth, dark green (scarlet red when ripe) chile ranges from mildly hot to very hot. *Jalapeños* generally are about 2 inches long, have rounded tips, and are quite popular because they're so easily seeded (the seeds and veins are very hot). In their dried form, *jalapeños* are known as *chipotles.*

Poblano Chile: This dark green chile with a mild, rich flavor is generally about 4 to 5 inches long, tapering from top to bottom in a triangular shape. *Pobla-*

nos are found in central Mexico, though they are now grown in the U.S. Southwest as well. In their dried state, they're known as *ancho* or *mulato* chiles.

Serrano Chile: A small (about 1 ½ inches-long), slightly pointed chile with a very hot, savory flavor. As it matures, its green skin turns bright red, then yellow. *Serranos* can be used fresh or cooked in various dishes such as guacamole and salsa. The dried *serrano* chile is called chile *seco* and is generally used in sauces.

Chiles at Dos Caminos

At Dos Caminos, we use a variety of chiles in our dishes. In guacamole, we use a combination of *jalapeños* and *serranos*. In our table sauces, we use *chiles de árbol*, *habaneros*, and *serranos*. We add dried chiles to many of our sauces, such as *pasillas* in the sauce for the Shrimp Empanadas and *mulato* and *ancho* chiles in *Mole Poblano*.

INGREDIENTS
INGREDIENTES

These are available online (see "Resources"), in most Latin grocery stores, and even in many supermarkets.

Achiote paste is a seasoning made from ground annatto seeds, spices, garlic, and vinegar or lime juice. It is popular in the Yucatán Peninsula.

Adobo, a tangy marinade or sauce commonly made with chiles, garlic, and vinegar along with tomatoes and spices, is used to season meat or poultry dishes.

Avocados are a staple of Mexican cooking. I prefer the California Hass variety with dark green bumpy skin because they are more flavorful and not watery. We use tons of them for our celebrated guacamole and as a garnish on many dishes.

Avocado leaves both dried and fresh are used as a seasoning in stocks, soups, and sauces. Their flavor is reminiscent of anise.

Banana leaves are quite pliant and used to wrap meat dishes, like lamb *barbacoa,* and tamales, especially in and around Oaxaca. They are sold frozen at specialty markets.

Boniato, or Caribbean sweet potatoes, have white flesh and dark rose-colored skin. They are not as sweet as other varieties, but may be used interchangeably.

Cajeta is the sinfully delicious Mexican version of *dulce de leche* that is preferably made with goat's milk slowly reduced with sugar into a thick caramel sauce. It is a specialty of Guanajuato and San Luis Potosí.

Canela, or Mexican cinnamon sticks, are softer in texture and milder tasting than American cinnamon that comes from *cassia* bark. It is also easier to grind.

Ceviche is traditionally made with a raw fish or shellfish that is "cooked" in citrus juice and mixed with other seasonings. Today, the term is sometimes extended to other foods, like fruit, as in our Strawberry-Lychee Raspado with Tropical Fruit Ceviche. For a longer discussion of ceviches, see page 110.

Chile powder can be made with a blend of several ground dried chiles or from just one variety, such as *ancho* or *chipotle*. They range from mild to fiery hot.

Chipotles en adobo are smoked *jalapeño* chiles packed in adobo sauce (see above) and canned. You will find them in many of my recipes.

Chorizo in Mexico, unlike Spanish or Portuguese sausage with the same name, is always purchased raw. The pork meat is seasoned with ground red chiles, paprika, and sometimes achiote, which give it its characteristic reddish color.

Cilantro is among the most commonly used herbs in Mexican cuisine. Both the stem and leaves are typically used. The plant was introduced into Mexico by Spanish conquerors; the seeds of the plant are called coriander.

Crema is Mexican sour cream. I like Media brand by Nestlé, which is readily available online. If you can't find it, mixing American sour cream thinned with heavy cream to a smoother consistency is a better solution than straight sour cream. You can also substitute *crème fraîche* or Greek yogurt in most recipes.

Epazote is an important Mexican culinary herb that tastes like a mix of mint, basil, and oregano. The long, jagged, pointy leaves become more assertive as the plant ages, so younger leaves are preferable. *Epazote* is a popular addition to bean dishes because it is said to reduce flatulence. Use oregano as a substitute.

Hoja Santa, or "holy leaf," is also known as "root beer plant." The aromatic herb smells somewhat like nutmeg or black pepper with a taste akin to anise or fresh tarragon. The large leaves are sometimes used to wrap tamales, fish, or poultry before cooking.

Huitlacoche (or Cuitlacoche) is a fungus that grows on ears of Mexican corn. During the growing season, the smoky-sweet flavored delicacy, also called "Mexican truffle" or "Mexican caviar," is frozen or canned for export if it is not eaten fresh.

Jamaica flowers are exquisite fuschia-colored blossoms of the hibiscus tree. When dried, they are used in beverages, like *agua de jamaica*, sorbets, and granitas.

Jicama is a crunchy, slightly sweet-tasting tuber known as Mexican potato. It has light brown skin and almost white flesh. To peel jicama, use a sharp paring knife to pull off the fibrous skin in sheets. It is easier than using a vegetable scraper.

Lard has long been the fat of choice in Mexican cuisine where it imparts a distinctive flavor to traditional preparations like *masa* for tamales. Americans now realize that lard makes pastry flaky and that it has less saturated fat than butter.

Maggi sauce is a condiment, much like Worcestershire sauce, that finds its way into many marinades, stews, and sauces. It is very salty, so just a dash is all you need.

Masa harina is cornmeal or corn flour typically sold in 1-kilo (2.2-pound) bags that are used for tamales and tortillas. I use Maseca brand. There are different grinds, from fine to coarse, as well as different colors, including blue. The term *masa* refers to any type of "dough"; it takes many forms including tortillas, tamales, and empanadas.

Mexican chocolate is coarsely ground with sugar and sometimes flavored with cinnamon, almonds, and vanilla. It is an essential ingredient in dark *mole* sauce. This rustic-style chocolate, most famously from the town of Oaxaca, is somewhat gritty in texture from the granulated sugar used in making it. It is not overly sweet. Stores sell the chocolate in cakes; the most popular brands are Ibarra and Abuelito. See page 246 for a longer history.

Mexican oregano is widely used in Mexican cuisine. It is usually purchased dried or in flakes and is slightly sweeter and a little stronger than Greek, Italian, or Sicilian varieties. It is readily available online.

Mixiotes are the outermost layers of young of maguey plant leaves called *pencas*. The membranes are removed in sheets and used to wrap little bundles of marinated meats and chiles, which are then steamed as you would tamales. Banana leaves, parchment paper, or even plastic sandwich bags wrapped in aluminum foil can be used instead.

Mole is a group of complex sauces made with many ingredients, including nuts, chiles, seeds, spices, fruits, and chocolate. Oaxaca and Puebla are the two centers of *mole* (page 29).

Nopales are paddles from young cactus plants. The needles are removed before they are marinated and grilled or used in other preparations (page 78).

Onions used in Mexican cooking are usually white; yellow ones may be substituted.

Pepitas are hulled dried pumpkin seeds that are central to *mole verde* and *pipian*.

Piloncillo is unrefined Mexican dark brown sugar sold in solid cone shapes with flattened tops. Sizes range from under an ounce to more than half a pound. At Dos Caminos, our *piloncillo* cones weigh 6 ounces apiece. While firmer in texture than American brown sugar, the two can be used interchangeably. However, *piloncillo* must be chopped with a serrated knife or grated before using.

Plantains are similar to bananas but starchier and less sweet. A plantain is ripe when it is black and soft. They are readily available today in supermarkets.

Queso Chihuahua is cheese made from cow's milk in the state of Chihuahua. One of the most popular Mexican cheeses, it is high in butterfat with a flavor similar to mild cheddar. When aged, it becomes tangy. It's typically used in chiles rellenos, Mexican-style fondue, and quesadillas. Good-quality Muenster or medium cheddar can be used in its place.

Queso Cotija is an aged, white, salty, crumbly cheese named for the town in Michoacán where it was first made. When heated, it softens but doesn't actually melt. It is similar to feta when fresh, or to Parmesan when aged. You can substitute feta, Romano, or Parmesan.

Queso fresco is fresh cheese (as the name indicates) made with cow's milk that is produced all over Mexico. Other local names include *queso de metate*, *queso molido*, and *queso ranchero*. The cheese is used fresh, as a table cheese, crumbled as a topping, or as a stuffing for chiles or quesadillas because it melts well. It has a pleasant acidity and creaminess.

Quesillo Oaxaca is from the Central Valley of Oaxaca; this whole cow's milk string cheese is creamy colored with a pleasantly acidic bite. Typically the cheese is sold as wound balls. It melts well and can be shredded and used to top appetizers or as a filling for quesadillas or chiles rellenos.

Queso requesón is similar to ricotta with a mild, somewhat sweet flavor. White, with a soft, moist texture, it is used in salads, tacos, cooked foods, and dessert.

Salt that is iodized, from my perspective, ruins the flavors of food. I suggest using either kosher or fine or coarse sea salt, as indicated by the recipe.

Tacos are usually fresh corn tortillas folded in half and filled with any combination of meat, cheese, vegetables, and condiments including tomatoes, lettuce, and salsa.

Tamales are made with corn tortilla dough; they are filled with meat, vegetables, or fruit, wrapped up in a cornhusk, and steamed.

Taquito is a little taco made of corn tortilla usually filled with meat, rolled up, and fried. It is a small version of the *flauta*.

Tamarind paste is the acidic-sweet tasting pulp surrounding the seeds of the tamarind pod. It has many uses, including in agua fresca, Tamarind Braised Short Ribs (page 191), and Tamarind Sorbet (page 231).

Tomatillos are members of the gooseberry family. They resemble a small green tomato with a papery husk that is removed before using. They are slightly tart but very flavorful; they are used in many sauces, especially green ones.

Tortillas are thin, circular disks of unleavened dough made of *masa* for corn tortillas or *harina* for flour tortillas. They are the most important item in Mexican cuisine.

Valentina Hot Sauce is my favorite brand of hot sauce, although there are plenty of other brands out there.

Yerba Buena is an herb in the mint family that is popular in Mexican cooking. Other mints can be substituted for it.

APPENDIX C
RESOURCES
RECURSOS

Internet

www.mexgrocer.com

The best for all-purpose shopping for Mexican ingredients.

Other sites include:

www.americanspice.com
www.gourmetsleuth.com
www.inmamaskitchen.com
www.thechileguy.com—for chiles
www.tazachocolate.com—for chocolate

Dried and canned chiles, masa harina, avocado leaves, Mexican chocolate, Mexican oregano, *achiote* paste, tortilla presses, comales, and hot sauces.

Mo Hotta Mo Betta
P.O. Box 4136
San Luis Obispo, CA 93403
800-462-3220

Mexican chocolate, Mexican cinnamon, pumpkin seeds, dried chiles, canned *chipotles*, pumpkin seeds, *masa harina*, hot sauces.

Mail Order

The CMC Company
P.O. Box 322
Avalon, NJ 08202
800-CMC-2780

INDEX